PERFUME & SCENT BOTTLE
COLLECTING
WITH PRICES

PERFUME & SCENT BOTTLE

C O L L E C T I N G

WITH PRICES

SECOND EDITION

JEAN SLOAN

Wallace-Homestead Book Company
Radnor, Pennsylvania

Designed by Anthony Jacobson
Drawings and photographs by Jean Sloan, unless otherwise credited
Perfume and scent bottles shown through the courtesy of identified owners, private
collectors, and The Glass House
Manufactured in the United States of America

Library of Congress Cataloging in Publication Data
Sloan, Jean.
     Perfume and scent bottle collecting, with prices / Jean L. Sloan.
          p.   cm.
     Includes bibliographical references.
     ISBN 0-87069-544-4 (alk. paper)
     1. Perfume bottles—Collectors and collecting—Catalogs.   2. Scent
bottles—Collectors and collecting—Catalogs.   I. Title.
NK5440.B6S56   1989
748.8'2'075—dc20   LC 89-50522
                                                               CIP

1 2 3 4 5 6 7 8 9 0   8 7 6 5 4 3 2 1 0 9

To my
family
and,
especially,
to the
newest
member,
Rachel

Contents

Preface   ix
Acknowledgments   xi
Introduction   1

1 A Brief Excursion into History   3

2 Vinaigrettes   9

3 European Scent Bottles   13

   Early Bristol   14
   Enamel Scent Bottles   16
   Treasures in Chests   16
   Sulphides   18
   The Fabulous French   20
   Double-Ended Scent Bottles   23
   Lithyalin and Hyalith Glass   26
   Dutch Scent Bottles   27

4 Early American Perfume and Scent Bottles   35

5 Chatelaines   41

6 Infinite Varieties   45

7 Smelling Salts   55

8 Cameo Glass   57

   English Cameo Glass   57
   French Cameo Glass   59
   Val St. Lambert   61

9 The Late Victorian Period   **63**

    Cut Glass 63
    Silver Overlay 69
    Sprinkler Top Perfumes 71
    Rings on Her Fingers 72
    The Glamour of Glitter 73
    "Mary Gregory" Glass 73

10 Big and Beautiful   **75**

11 The Innovators   **79**

    Lalique 79
    Louis Comfort Tiffany 83
    Frederick Carder 84
    Thomas Webb 85
    Fabergé and Ovchinnikov 85
    Ludwig Moser and Son 86
    Josiah Wedgwood 87
    John Turner 88
    French Enameled Scents 88

12 DeVilbiss   **91**

13 Commercial Perfume Bottles   **119**

14 Czechoslovakian Perfume Bottles   **127**

15 An Assortment from the Twentieth Century   **135**

    Dime Store Novelties 140
    Contemporary Art Glass 141

16 How to Shop for Perfume and Scent Bottles   **145**

17 How to Display a Collection   **149**

Glossary   **153**
Bibliography   **157**
Museums   **161**
Index   **163**
Price Guide   **168**

Preface

After *Perfume and Scent Bottle Collecting* came out in 1986 and was so warmly received, friends and customers from all over asked for a larger book with more pictures. I was in favor of this, too; however, I could not think of a way to write an entirely new book and still maintain the pertinent information contained in the original. Therefore, I have added new material all through the second edition of *Perfume and Scent Bottle Collecting* along with a great many illustrations, and I hope it will be looked upon as a text for study and not the end-all and-be-all of scent container collecting. I hope this book will be a springboard for further study and will create new fields of interest for the reader.

The popularity of this area of collecting has become so intense in recent years that a number of books, mentioned in the bibliography, have been published in the United States and Europe. A perfume bottle collecting club was formed in the United States and its membership grew to more than three hundred in the first year! In Scotland, a museum for perfumery was established, opening in 1989.

Often I have been asked, "Why did you start collecting perfume bottles?" I have to honestly admit, I do not collect. Not that I have anything against collecting, but, as an antiques dealer, I feel it is not good business to compete with my customers. There are many bottles that I would never have been able to part with had I been a collector. However, my business partner (who also happens to be my husband, Charles) and I have the fun of seeking out these rare treasures, researching and identifying them, and photographing them for our records and for use as visual aids when we are asked to give talks to groups. As it turned out, we used a great deal of this material for *Perfume and Scent Bottle Collecting.* We also have the pleasure of turning the bottles over to collectors who are going to cherish them for the wonderful things they are, not to mention the investment potential they may possess.

What started my considerable interest in this field of collection was seeing a group of DeVilbiss and other perfume bottles from the 1920s displayed for sale by another antiques dealer at one of the first antique shows in which we exhibited. Charles and I are dealers in American and European glass from the eighteenth and early nineteenth centuries and in business as The Glass House. Somehow, this display of charming perfume bottles excited me so much that I bought every one of them, not really knowing what I had. It was then that I discovered there was little to read on the subject, particularly on American bottles of the twentieth century.

Research for this second edition has been compiled by gleaning information from books on glass, porcelain, silver, and antiques, along with magazine articles, interviews, and by searching through museums. We hope this book answers questions for the reader concerning perfume and scent bottle collecting. If it helps the collector gain more knowledge and pleasure in his or her collecting, then it will have been a success.

Acknowledgments

Special thanks to the following wonderful people for allowing their collections to be photographed and for the encouragement and interest they have taken in the writing of this book: Fran Peters, Arleta Rodrigues, Rita M. Kondos, Jody Speer, and other good friends. By sharing their treasures, many that are one-of-a-kind, they have added to the pleasure and knowledge of all who are interested in perfume and scent bottles.

It would be impossible to mention all the people who have helped, inspired, and given me the impetus to write the first book and now this second edition. This is just a word of appreciation to tell them that they are very special and how happy I am our friendships have grown over the years. Thanks to Joyce Geeser, Jim and Barbara Gomes, Madeleine France, Elsa Tolchiner, Elizabeth Creech, Ellen Foster, Suzanne Wylie, and to the countless thoughtful people who have written, called, or stopped in at antique shows and on other occasions to pass on kind remarks. You are all wonderful.

For cooperation in permitting research in their libraries or of their records, I wish to thank the following:

The DeVilbiss Company, Health Care Division, Somerset, Pennsylvania (formerly Toledo, Ohio), for allowing the reprinting of their catalog and for their kind help.

The Victoria and Albert Museum, London, England.

The City of Bristol Museum & Art Gallery, Bristol, England.

The Fragrance Foundation, New York, New York.

The Corning Museum of Glass, Corning, New York.

The State Historical Society, Madison, Wisconsin.

A very special thanks goes to the University of Wisconsin for allowing me to research for countless hours at the University of Wisconsin Library (particularly the Kohler Art Library) and at the Elvehjem Museum of Art, Madison.

The Madison Public Library made microfilmed books available that furnished research information vital to the writing of this book.

PERFUME &
SCENT BOTTLE
COLLECTING

WITH PRICES

Introduction

The exact date, or even century, that people began to use scents to enhance the human body is still a secret. Some of the first perfume vials in existence date from the early Egyptian and Roman civilizations. Vials were placed in tombs as offerings to the gods and as accessories to accompany the deceased on their journeys into the future world. Most were made of pottery or carved from stone, such as alabaster or onyx. By the second or first centuries B.C., tiny, hand-blown glass bottles were being used to hold precious fragrances.

We know that the techniques of extracting essences from flowers, oils, trees, roots, and, of course, animals were discovered many centuries ago. The essential oils from these sources were beaten, squeezed, steamed, aged, and mixed until just the right blend was achieved. The processes have become more sophisticated and controlled, with many synthetic scents replacing the natural compounds, but perfumes of some sort are probably here to stay.

Scents, in whatever form they took, be it liquid, cream, powder, oil, or solid, had to be housed in containers of some sort to protect and store them. Scent containers were luxury items, given to and created for deities, royalty, the aristocracy, and the wealthy. It naturally follows that the finest artisans and craftsmen would be occupied with their manufacture, but certainly the poorer classes must have used scents of some kind also. Perhaps these were concocted at home, and the vessels to hold them were probably made of leather, pottery, or metal. However, only the best examples have survived over the centuries, so we have little record of the type of bottles used by the less privileged. From the Dark Ages following the fall of the Roman Empire, little evidence remains of the use of perfumes and their containers; accordingly, that period will not be discussed in this book.

It was only in the last half of the nineteenth century that scented products became available to everyone in all walks of life. The Industrial Revolution brought with it new techniques in manufacture, new materials, and a working class that could afford a touch of luxury. Perfume was one of these luxuries.

Why are the containers called scent and perfume bottles? The reason is because they were used for carrying both perfumes and scented oils and, most importantly, smelling salts. In this book, the term scent bottle will designate those bottles made prior to 1900, especially the smaller lay-down bottles or those that could conceivably have been used for smelling salts (which could also be pleasantly scented).

In the United States, we can rejoice that our society has its roots in so many cultures. This diversity of backgrounds makes the collecting of perfume containers from many countries all the more exciting.

With this book, it is my hope that you will become more aware of the broad spectrum of perfume and scent bottles. I hope it will help you search, identify, and make your purchases with greater knowledge and selectivity. Most of all, I hope that it will help you develop a greater appreciation of origins, quality, and value. *Note:* The measurements attributed to the bottles pictured are sometimes approximate.

1

A Brief Excursion into History

The chance of a collector coming upon early Greek or Roman scent flasks today is slight. Those made of terra-cotta can be seen only in museums and private collections and seldom come into the auction houses or salesrooms.

Since most small bottles were unguent or perfume related, the collector will be more likely to find a glass vial from those early days, and this would be considered a rare addition to a collection.

The first glass bottles were made with the sand core method, wherein a mold made of sand was attached to a metal rod. Then glass, while still in the molten stage, was wound around the core in threads. In another method, a

Fig. 1—1

Early Syrian and Grecian containers.

Fig. 1–2

Blown glass scent bottle, mouse-shaped with applied details, dates from Roman Empire period, c. 300–400 A.D. From eastern Mediterranean area, possibly Egyptian workmanship. Courtesy of the Corning Museum of Glass.

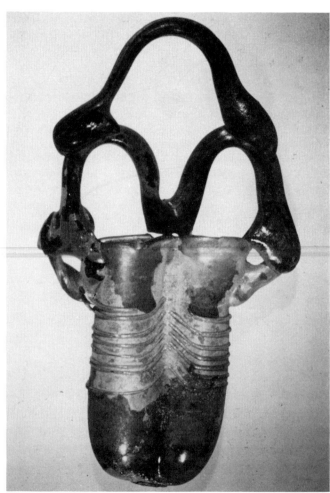

Fig. 1–3

Double unguentarium from Roman Empire period, c. 300–400 A.D., is blown glass with applied details. Courtesy of the Corning Museum of Glass.

Fig. 1–4

Roman Empire scent flask, c. 100 A.D., was mold blown. Courtesy of the Corning Museum of Glass.

Fig. 1–5

Pouncet, or smelling box, in hand-tooled silver with gold crown, was made c. 1800. Engraved on the bottom at a later date, "K HC & DK, 1844." Hallmarks are quite worn and rough but appear to read, "Hamm, Germany."

sand mold was dipped into the hot glass and, when cooled, the mold was removed, leaving a glass shell. The Greeks began to blow glass in the second century B.C.

Some bottles were made in the shapes of birds or fish, and some resembled human heads. The most common style was tubular, probably because it was the simplest to make. Bottles were made as single flacons, or sometimes two were joined by decorative glass ribbons in clear or opaque colors. The Romans brought more sophistication to glassmaking and developed the art of layering one color of glass over another, which allowed decoration by cutting in cameo style.

We know very little about glassmaking in the Dark Ages. In Christian Europe, the manufacture of glass almost disappeared during this time. It is generally supposed that pottery and metal and, to a lesser degree, wood and leather containers were used because household equipment of the period was made of these materials.

At the beginning of the Renaissance in 1500 A.D., it became fashionable for those who were concerned about sanitation and odors to carry fragrant pomanders made from oranges pierced with cloves and treated with other spices.

Fig. 1—6

Silversmith's pomander.

Fig. 1–7

Smelling box, Scandinavian, c. 1800. Legend tells these were often filled with gold coins and given to a bride on her wedding day. After the coins were removed, she could carry the box with a scented sponge within.

The pomander idea was adopted by silversmiths who created handsome boxes in the shapes of oranges, apples, or other fruits. These boxes opened in segments to reveal a variety of solid scents, such as essences of clove, cinnamon, nutmeg, and others. The pomander was widely used until the invention of the pouncet, or sponge box.

Pouncet boxes became popular with the privileged classes throughout Europe in the sixteenth century. Made of gold and silver and occasionally jeweled, they were circular, oblong, or heart-shaped and often had pedestal-type feet. Lift-off or hinged lids opened to reveal a sponge that could be soaked in a perfumed vinegar. Lids sometimes were made with holes to enable the owner to sniff the fragrance without removing the top. These boxes often had a compartment in the foot where a small amount of musk might be hidden. Gold or silver pouncet boxes were engraved with emblems, initials, heraldic devices, or other decorative motifs.

2

Vinaigrettes

Vinaigrettes supplanted pouncet boxes in the last quarter of the eighteenth century. They became so popular throughout Britain and the Continent that goldsmiths and silversmiths, lapidaries, and jewelers were kept busy turning out exciting, imaginative pieces to meet the demands. Usually vinaigrettes were very small, measuring about $\frac{3}{4}''$ wide and $\frac{1}{4}''$ deep. Even the larger, double containers of the mid-Victorian period were only 3″ to 4″ long. The vinaigrette could be very plain, but that was the exception. Most often, the decoration was a deep repoussé, machine-turned, or engraved. Occasionally gold was inlaid into the silver, or jewels were mounted into the metal. Enameled containers were also made, usually by Continental European artists. Some were egg-shaped while other shapes featured delicately painted miniature scenes to pleasure the eye of the owner.

Of great interest to the collector is the inner grille of a vinaigrette. Most are more intricate in design than the outer box. This piece of metal, sometimes of solid gold but often of silver with a heavy gold coating, might be cut into flowers, scrolls, or initials. Seldom was it merely worked with pierced holes. Gold was used because it resisted the corroding effect of the acid-containing liquids in the sponge under the grille.

Bloodstone, agate, jade, and other semiprecious stones were sometimes used instead of metal for the wee container.

The vinaigrettes were made in the forms of animals, purses, watches, or whatever the imagination could contrive. Some were fashioned with tiny rings attached to one end to enable the wearer to hang it from a chatelaine hook or watch chain. They were also made into rings and pendants (Fig. C-36).

Fig. 2–1

Left: *Norwegian vinaigrette, c. 1840.* Center and lower right: *English silver.* Upper right: *Two cut glass and silver pieces. English, first quarter of the nineteenth century.* Photograph: Skylight Studio.

Fig. 2–2

Upper left: *Rare watch fob scent bottle intricately molded in solid silver and suspended on a silver chain with solid gold links. Probably European, c. 1850. Bottom left: Vinaigrette with machined decoration in center panel framed by deep repoussé, from Birmingham, England, 1850. Center: Vinaigrette with an ornate grid shaped with soldered wires and plated in gold, from Birmingham, England, 1823. Right: Egg-shaped vinaigrette in silver-plated copper. Grid unscrews to enable user to fill it. The cap also unscrews, as does the very bottom, revealing a tiny, hidden compartment where possibly a solid piece of musk was carried. From the Continent, first half of nineteenth century, $\frac{3}{4}$″ (2 cm) long.*

Fig. 2–3

Vinaigrette in shape of a horn. Made of ruby-colored glass cut in shallow diamonds and mounted on each end in silver gilt. A grid on large end with hinged cap and hinged cap on other end for perfume or smelling salts. Probably England, c. 1840, $3\frac{1}{2}$″ (8.8 cm).

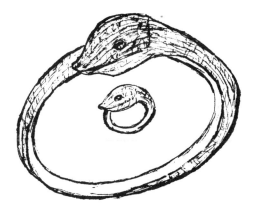

Fig. 2–4

Vinaigrette bracelet and ring set.

More unusual are the glass vinaigrettes of the first half of the nineteenth century. Minute bottles were blown and/or cut, often with painstakingly intricate designs, and mounted with silver or gold necks and caps. The grille over the mouth of the bottle sometimes had simple holes pierced into the metal, but more often elaborate designs were cut into it. The cap was probably worked in fine repoussé to complement the inner grille. Both could be unscrewed from the bottle.

The vinaigrette served several purposes. It was not only used for sniffing, in the event the owner was confronted with an unpleasant odor, but also its sponge could be removed and the scent applied to the body. The fragrance was supposed to make one more delightful to be near, and the vinegar was believed to have healing qualities when applied to sores and other skin eruptions.

The lengths to which a jeweler might go to create an outstanding vinaigrette knew no bounds. For instance, a ring and bracelet set crafted around 1800 was made in the shapes of coiled snakes. The bracelet was gold with tiny, baguette-cut emeralds covering the top of the bracelet to form a sparkling green skin. The head that grasped the tail had ruby eyes and sapphire accents. The serpent's mouth opened to reveal a tiny grid. The matching ring had an even more miniscule vinaigrette concealed in its serpent's head. Rare jewelry such as this commanded a great price when it was made and is very highly valued today.

Although dainty vinaigrettes were made in Scotland, often much larger pieces were created than those found in England and Europe. Animal horn was used, and these closely resembled the popular snuff mulls and were miniature versions of the dress parade powder horns. Some were made in the shape of a horn from stone or other material.

Like the snuff mulls, the vinaigrettes were mounted with heavy silver that was usually tooled in Scottish symbols, the thistle being one of the most popular (Fig. 2–5). Semi-precious stones, the amber-colored cairngorm being most popular, were cut and fitted into the mountings, and chains with rings were added to enable the user to wear it as a decorative piece of jewelry. Occasionally, they were made of stone, such as agate. Some vinaigrettes were made of silver inlaid with semiprecious stones.

Fig. 2–5

Two wonderful vinaigrettes from nineteenth-century Scotland. On the left is a green agate, horn-shaped piece. The heavy silver mount is deeply tooled with thistles. The stones are faceted cairngorms. On the right is a genuine horn vinaigrette. The silver is also lavishly decorated with thistles. Quartz crystal stones decorate both ends. About 5" (12.5 cm), each vinaigrette has a handmade silver chain with ring (see Fig. C-9).

3

European Scent Bottles

The European artisans of the eighteenth and nineteenth centuries who designed and crafted scent bottles were limited in form only by their imagination. A wide variety of materials was available to them—porcelain, silver, gold, brass, wood, tortoiseshell, pearl, gemstones, ivory, stone, and more.

However, glass was, and is, the most common substance used for scent bottles. Because of its impermeable quality, odors cannot escape and air cannot affect the contents if the glass is sealed properly. Then, too, an amazing variety and beauty can be achieved by the glass manufacturer.

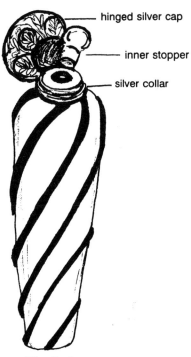

The most beautiful antique perfume containers are from the British Isles and the Continent because Europe had a large and wealthy aristocratic class that could demand rare, magnificent, and expensive luxuries. Usually, the bottles were hand blown in one color of glass then cut, engraved, or enameled. The more complex designs could entail the use of one or two additional layers of colored glass overlaying the original base. Intricate designs could be worked through these layers. Finally, a small hole was drilled into the neck to receive the equally tiny stopper ground to fit it perfectly. Bottles were often mounted with a neck ring and cap of precious metal or brass.

hinged silver cap

inner stopper

silver collar

Fig. 3–1

Early Bristol

English cobalt blue glass is celebrated among collectors because of the richness and depth of its color. Fine wine glasses, decanters, and other tableware were made in cobalt blue glass, but the most charming pieces to the perfume and scent bottle collector are the delicate, miniature bottles created to enclose scents of all kinds (Fig. 3–2).

Because glass was being made in Bristol, England, in the eighteenth and early nineteenth centuries, Bristol has become a generic term for much of the early English glass made at that time, particularly in cobalt blue, green, white, and red. However, not all pieces were really made in Bristol. When the term is used in this book, it could refer to glass made in Bristol or London or elsewhere in England during that period.

Fig. 3–2

Eighteenth-century cobalt scent bottles. Courtesy of the City of Bristol Museum & Art Gallery, Bristol, England.

There was also a so-called Bristol glass produced in the late years of the nineteenth century. This glass generally was crudely made, brightly enameled, and formed into large dresser items, such as colognes. It did not possess the artistic merits of the early Bristol glass. Much of this late Victorian glass was not even made in England—let alone in Bristol.

Two excellent examples of Bristol blue scent bottles are shown in Fig. 3–2. At the left is a six-sided, urn-shaped bottle with a pedestal foot. The foot is cut in scallops and the bottle cut in angular planes at the shoulder that curve up the neck. The stopper, which resembles a gilded flame, is held on the bottle by a gold chain. The intricate gold decoration in random floral motifs and popular eighteenth-century adornments was applied by hand. It is not certain if this or the bottle on its right was made in Bristol or in London.

The other fine bottle of Bristol blue has shallow cut diamonds gracing the entire surface. Beautifully painted in gold, it depicts a gentleman in a tricorn hat seated beneath a tree.

As early as the mid-1700s in Bristol, glassmakers were experimenting with white glass in attempts to duplicate the look of porcelain. The glass was decorated by cutting and enameling. Two outstanding examples from the late eighteenth century in opaque white are shown in Fig. 3–3. The flat oval bottle

Fig. 3–3

Eighteenth-century opaque white scent bottles. Courtesy of the City of Bristol Museum & Art Gallery, Bristol, England.

is decorated in the popular chinoiserie style of the period. Gold was lavishly used to emphasize the contours. Each small oval cut on the sides of the bottle is trimmed in an oval bull's-eye. Elongated diamonds also trim the sides. On the front panel is a pagoda with trees and birds flying overhead. The mounting is hand engraved and bright cut silver gilt. The other bottle has a flat front and simple, slightly scalloped sides with allover, hand-painted gilding. The front panel has a stylized floral pattern. The neck is ringed with gold, and the stopper of white glass is also decorated in gold.

These four fine bottles can be seen at the City of Bristol Museum & Art Gallery, Bristol, England. Naturally, early scent bottles such as these are not easily found, particularly in the United States. However, if one keeps a sharp eye at antique shops and shows, one of these excellent pieces of antiquity could be found to add to a collection.

Enamel Scent Bottles

For those who prize rare scent bottles, a wonderful enameled piece would be a delightful addition. The eighteenth and nineteenth centuries found enamelers creating exquisite jewelry, snuffboxes, trinket boxes, scent bottles, and other imaginative items. Enameling on copper was developed in the Germanic area of Europe. Talented artists were hired to paint scenes inspired by known masterworks.

At Limoges, France, scent bottles were often decorated in the style of Boucher and Fragonard showing the aristocracy dressed as country people in idealized bucolic scenes.

Most enameled pieces were created for the wealthy to give and receive as gifts. However, in England not only were extremely fine and costly pieces made but inexpensive boxes and other items bearing printed greetings and slogans were produced at Bilston that could be purchased by the common folk.

Treasures in Chests

Scent bottles also came in sets, and often they were protected by handsomely fitted cases. Three hand-blown cobalt blue bottles with cut and polished straight

Figs. 3–4 and 3–5

A magnificent box of bronze doré in Empire design. On the lid are applied cornucopias; the sides and bottom are heavy and deeply cut topaz-colored glass. Tiny hooves support it all. Within are six wee rectangular bottles also of cut topaz glass and mounted with vermeil caps. Two ornate vermeil (silver gilt) funnels rest between the bottles. The tiny gilded key rests below. French, c. 1825.

sides and matching square-cut stoppers are shown in Fig. 3–6. Gold was applied to the sloping shoulders and on the stoppers in delicate tracery. The case is ebonized wood inlaid with brass strips and with a cut brass medallion on the top that reveals mother-of-pearl beneath. The case is lined in white silk moiré taffeta. It retains its original key to protect the precious contents. The case is 6″ long, 5″ high, and 3″ deep (15 cm × 12.5 cm × 7.5 cm). It probably was made in England during the first quarter of the eighteenth century.

On the right in Fig. 3–6 are two white opaline bottles mounted in gilded brass with miniature prints of Paris street scenes framed under glass in the caps. The bottles have ground inner stoppers and a gold star motif. The wooden casket has excellent brass bindings with intricate engravings repeated in the key escutcheon. It is lined in deep green velvet. It also has its original key. This was made in France during the mid-nineteenth century.

Fig. 3–6

Left: *English cobalt blue bottles in ebonized case.* Right: *French opaline bottles in wooden chest.* Center: *Clear French bottles in mother-of-pearl and ormolu casket.*

In the foreground of Fig. 3–6 is a dainty pair of hand-blown, clear glass bottles mounted in ormolu, with intricate work around the shoulders. The caps have glass inserts with reverse paintings of stylized flowers, and mother-of-pearl reflects from beneath. The handled case is covered in strips of mother-of-pearl and tortoiseshell, with ormolu strapping in a Greek key design accented in white and blue enamel; made in France during the first quarter of the nineteenth century. Figs. 3–7 and 3–8 show additional chests.

Sulphides

This difficult-to-produce decorative glass is made by inserting portraits, emblems, or other shapes made of fired clay between two layers of glass. Items made by this procedure are called "sulphides," "crystallo-ceramie," or "cameo incrustations."

Early glassmakers had problems creating these pieces. It was difficult to achieve a mixture of clay and other materials for the cameo that would retain its shape in the higher temperature of the glass envelope into which it was inserted. Stabilizing the two substances, the glass and the encrustation, was a serious problem for the glassmaker. He had to find a combination of materials that would produce the proper coefficient of expansion and not crack in the process of annealing. Not only was that a problem, but there was a real danger to the glassblower himself. After making the pocket or envelope in the molten glass and inserting the cameo, he had to withdraw the air from the pocket by sucking on the blowpipe!

Fig. C-1

Three bottles with interior colors of amber, blue, and amethyst, all acid-etched. They were made by Gary Genetti in the late twentieth century. Courtesy of D. Erlien Fine arts, Milwaukee, Wisconsin. Photograph by Linda Erlien.

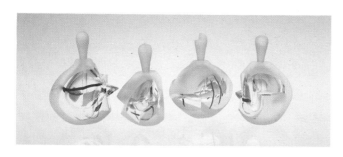

Fig. C-2

Four free-form bottles, frosted and cut at daring angles by Joseph Kilvin III. American; late twentieth century; about $3\frac{1}{2}''$ (9cm) tall. Courtesy of D. Erlien Fine Arts, Milwaukee, Wisconsin. Photograph by Linda Erlien.

Fig. C-3

Three blown bottles, clear glass with red accents. They were created at the studios of The Glass House, Seattle, Washington, late twentieth century. Tallest about 5" (12.5cm). Courtesy of D. Erlien Fine Arts, Milwaukee, Wisconsin. Photograph by Linda Erlien.

Fig. C-4

Four bottles in flattened apple shape, accented in blues and red. Blown by S.I.N., late twentieth century. The bottles are about $3\frac{1}{2}''$ (9cm) tall. Courtesy of D. Erlien Fine Arts, Milwaukee, Wisconsin. Photograph by Linda Erlien.

Fig. C-5

Fig. C-6

Fig. C-7

Fig. C-5 A three-piece set consisting of two large scent bottles and a powder jar. All porcelain pieces have ormolu mountings. The two bottles have beautifully painted scenes of lovers in country settings on the front and back. The powder jar has a similar scene on the hinged lid, plus flowers. The set is European, probably Germanic, nineteenth century.

Fig. C-6 Porcelain double-ended scent bottle set with silver screw-on mounts. Deep blue and white are set off by the red flowers and gold trim. England, second half of the nineteenth century, $3\frac{3}{4}''$ (9cm) long.

Fig. C-7 A porcelain figurine of a woman wearing an eighteenth-century court costume and wig of northern Europe. There is a hole in the top of the head to accommodate a tiny plume, which was the fashion. The person depicted is assumed to be the empress of Poland, who reigned from 1770 to 1790, due to the similarity of features, dress, and wig. The head is the stopper. Unmarked, it is $4\frac{1}{2}''$ (11cm) tall.

Fig. C-8

Fig. C-9

Fig. C-10

Fig. C-8 A lovely bottle with a most unusual cut. Note the step cuts on the shoulder and left side; on the right side, prism cuts radiate from the center. The stopper is round facet cut. Probably American, second half of the nineteenth century.

Fig. C-9 A handsome double-ended scent bottle made of banded agate and silver. On the top is a snap-top scent bottle with a chain and ring attached to it. On the base is a cover that reveals a vinaigrette with a silver gilt grid when opened. England, fourth quarter of the nineteenth century; about 3" (7.5cm) tall.

Fig. C-10 A tapered silver overlay bottle in clear glass; about 5½" (13.5cm) tall; American. At right is a bottle cut in the cane pattern with a hand-tooled sterling silver cap.

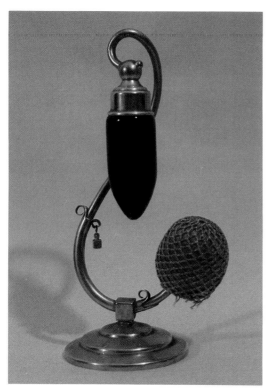

Fig. C-11

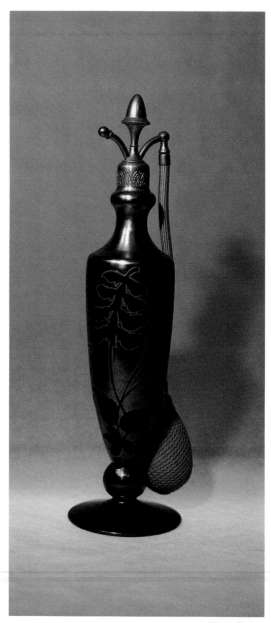

Fig. C-12

Fig. C-13

Fig. C-11 *From the "Debutante" series by DeVilbiss. A black bullet-shaped bottle is suspended from the spiral tubing that ends with the squeeze bulb. A whimsical dangle hangs from a curl of metal; c. 1927; about 6" (15cm) high.*

Fig. C-12 *A rare, beautiful, and unusually large blue Steuben Aurene bottle made for DeVilbiss. Urn shape with a round knob at the base. Cut in large shallow leaf design by Hawkes; c. 1925; 11½" (29cm) tall.*

Fig. C-13 *Superb porcelain bottle, glazed in pink with ovals on each side glazed in soft grays, browns, and pinks to resemble an evening sky in a craquelle finish. Gold is lavishly used all over, and along the right and left sides are tiny enamel turquoise "jewels." The handsome metalware is silver gilt. Made by Coalport, 1893; 4¾" (12cm) long.*

Fig. C-16

Fig. C-17

Fig. C-14

Fig. C-15

Fig. C-14 *Two American cologne bottles from the mid-nineteenth century attributed to the Boston and Sandwich Glass Company. The amethyst twelve-sided bottle is dwarfed by the very tall bottle, about 10″ (25cm), of extremely rare colors, shading from a dark brown at the base and neck to an amber color in the middle.*

Fig. C-15 *Probably a rare, genuine Mary Gregory-painted bottle. Hand-blown lead glass, cut and polished, with a facet-cut stopper by the Boston and Sandwich Glass Company, c. 1890. The bottle is painted on all four sides: the front has a winter farmyard scene; various weeds and twigs in the snow appear on other sides. About 6″ (15cm) tall.*

Fig. C-16 *Three scent bottles from the nineteenth century. Left to right: A clear bottle with silver filigree encasing it and aqua stones on the cap and sides; probably French, late 1800s. Green opalene bottle decorated with minute gold stars; the cap and chain are brass; French, c. 1840. A very unusual bottle of opaque amber; the collar, bottom, and top finials are solid gold with fine turquoise set into them; the bottle is lined with silver to hold a wee amount of perfume; probably from the Middle East.*

Fig. C-17 *Unusual sea horse scent bottle, white with colored canes of blue, yellow, and purple. Rigaree well laid on to decorate edges. It would have had a cork stopper. Probably American, late eighteenth to early nineteenth centuries, 3″ (7.5cm) long.*

Fig. C-18

Fig. C-19

Fig. C-20

Fig. C-18 *The flapper era is well represented by this three-piece porcelain set from Bavaria. The powder box has a saucy girl perched on top of it, while the two perfume girls pull out from the bottles at the waistlines. The bottles and box are light blue with dark blue chevrons, and the girl on the box wears a yellow dress. About 6" (15cm) high.*

Fig. C-19 *A nice three-piece porcelain set made in Bavaria. The torso tops (with long glass droppers attached to cork stoppers) pull apart above the hobble skirts. They and the matching powder box are glazed in mottled pale yellow. These sets were quite popular in the first quarter of the twentieth century. The bottles are 7" (18cm) high.*

Fig. C-20 *Czechoslovakian Deco bottle in pale olive-green glass; parallelogram shape, with the stopper carrying out the same angles. Filigree with red cut stones is juxtaposed against the stern sharp lines; about 4" (10cm).*

Fig. C-16

Fig. C-17

Fig. C-14

Fig. C-15

Fig. C-14 *Two American cologne bottles from the mid-nineteenth century attributed to the Boston and Sandwich Glass Company. The amethyst twelve-sided bottle is dwarfed by the very tall bottle, about 10" (25cm), of extremely rare colors, shading from a dark brown at the base and neck to an amber color in the middle.*

Fig. C-15 *Probably a rare, genuine Mary Gregory-painted bottle. Hand-blown lead glass, cut and polished, with a facet-cut stopper by the Boston and Sandwich Glass Company, c. 1890. The bottle is painted on all four sides: the front has a winter farmyard scene; various weeds and twigs in the snow appear on other sides. About 6" (15cm) tall.*

Fig. C-16 *Three scent bottles from the nineteenth century. Left to right: A clear bottle with silver filigree encasing it and aqua stones on the cap and sides; probably French, late 1800s. Green opalene bottle decorated with minute gold stars; the cap and chain are brass; French, c. 1840. A very unusual bottle of opaque amber; the collar, bottom, and top finials are solid gold with fine turquoise set into them; the bottle is lined with silver to hold a wee amount of perfume; probably from the Middle East.*

Fig. C-17 *Unusual sea horse scent bottle, white with colored canes of blue, yellow, and purple. Rigaree well laid on to decorate edges. It would have had a cork stopper. Probably American, late eighteenth to early nineteenth centuries, 3" (7.5cm) long.*

Fig. C-18

Fig. C-19

Fig. C-20

Fig. C-18 *The flapper era is well represented by this three-piece porcelain set from Bavaria. The powder box has a saucy girl perched on top of it, while the two perfume girls pull out from the bottles at the waistlines. The bottles and box are light blue with dark blue chevrons, and the girl on the box wears a yellow dress. About 6" (15cm) high.*

Fig. C-19 *A nice three-piece porcelain set made in Bavaria. The torso tops (with long glass droppers attached to cork stoppers) pull apart above the hobble skirts. They and the matching powder box are glazed in mottled pale yellow. These sets were quite popular in the first quarter of the twentieth century. The bottles are 7" (18cm) high.*

Fig. C-20 *Czechoslovakian Deco bottle in pale olive-green glass; parallelogram shape, with the stopper carrying out the same angles. Filigree with red cut stones is juxtaposed against the stern sharp lines; about 4" (10cm).*

Fig. C-21

Fig. C-22

Fig. C-23

Figs. C-21 and **C-22** *Deep violet-colored bottle, simply cut, engraved on one side with a royal crest and the date "1824", on the other side are engraved a sword, scepter, crown, and the script initials "L. N." It is believed to be the personal scent bottle of Louis Napoleón. The engravings are emphasized by the use of gold. The stopper is pewter with a long, carved camphor wood dauber. It is 6" (15cm) long.*

Fig. C-23 *Two bottles of amethyst glass over clear, intricately cut in tiny geometrics and extraordinarily long at 11" (29cm). They are mounted with brass fittings and rest in a brass holder. Probably French, the fourth quarter of the nineteenth century.*

Fig. C-24 *An assortment of sterling silver scent bottles, all American except for the round one in the center (England). At the left is a bottle from Tiffany's in an amphora shape, c. 1865. At center top is a deep repoussé, c. 1870. At right is a very heavy, pointed amphora type with bright cutwork against a stippled background; a heavy chain connects the bottle to the chatelaine hook with its finely worked shield-shaped front piece. Below, another similarly shaped bottle with a chain; it has a bright cut floral motif.*

Nevertheless, the process was mastered, and, during the first half of the nineteenth century, sulphides were produced in all conceivable forms and sizes. Scent bottles (or smelling bottles, as they were sometimes called) were also made. Due to the rarity of early sulphides in any form, sulphide scent or cologne bottles are especially valuable.

Some of the recognized pioneers in sulphides are Honare and Boudon de St. Amans of France and Apsley Pellatt of England. Pellatt found that a

Fig. 3—8

Three blown bottles with polished sides, rounded shoulders, and square cut and beveled stoppers are trimmed with hand-applied gold floral designs. Imprinted on one label is: "Wright's Double Extract, Jockey Club, for the Handkerchief." The other two labels bear the same logo except for "Jockey Club." Instead, written in ink with beautiful penmanship on one is the name, "Mrs. Monroe Hay," and on the other, "Sweet Pink." The bottles rest in a red silk-lined interior. The ebony-finished box is inlaid with strips of brass and an inset cartouche engraved, "Carrie's, June 28, 1852," The case is 6" (15 cm) long, 3½" (9 cm) high. Made in England.

combination of china clay and super silicate of potash was able to withstand the intense heat during firing and the quick cooling afterward. Sulphides are being made today, usually in the form of paperweights, but they seem to lack the lustrous quality the early sulphides possessed.

Still in very fine condition and shown on the left in Fig. 3–9, is a sulphide bottle with an excellent portrait of William I, king of the Netherlands, signed in ink on the bottom of the bust and readable from the front. On the back, seen through the bottle, are the large letters, "M.T." The glass is hand cut about the sides, and the silver mounting is impressed with the Paris guarantee mark, 1817–1838. The bottle was made at the Baccarat factory. It is $2\frac{3}{4}''$ (7 cm) tall.

To the right in the photograph is a bottle that is earlier, from around 1800, with a portrait cameo mounted on the outside of the bottle. The bottle is nicely cut and has a silver cap marked on the top with the letter "R" in a circle. This is not a true sulphide since the cameo appears to be made of opaque glass and is not imbedded within the glass. This bottle was made in England or Ireland.

The Fabulous French

For utterly romantic presentations of scent bottles, it seems no other country could compare to France.

Not only did the French dominate in the use of bronze doré and brass to make beautiful holders in which the pretty bottles would be fitted—many in the classic Grecian style of the Empire period—but they used tooled metal cut in lacy patterns to decorate the shoulders of the bottles. The hinged caps had recessed tops, and into these were fitted minute hand-painted portraits, reverse paintings of tourist attractions, tiny hand-colored engravings (all protected under tiny glass disks), or hand-painted porcelain inserts.

The French wove bronze wires and ormolu strips into shapes of baskets, beehives, or whatever their imaginations could conceive. They made tiny animals with harnesses that would forever pull their fragrant burdens nestled in whimsical vehicles (Fig. C-26).

A very handsome and clever container was made of rosewood in the first half of the nineteenth century that had three round compartments that opened when the ormolu parrot finial was turned. When opened, three little bottles were revealed—one blue, one white, and one cranberry with gold trim—that sat in velvet restraints in each corner. The inner gears and shaft were made entirely of wood.

The twelve bottles in Fig. 3–10 illustrate some of the varieties that were made in Europe in the nineteenth century. The delicacy of cutting is evident in the top row of bottles and in the bottle on the right in the second row.

The bottle in the top row, at the far left, is a rich amethyst glass over clear, deeply cut with a fine, hand-worked silver mounting. Next is a three-layered glass bottle, cut through to reveal pink over white over clear, in trefoil and quatrefoil designs and mounted in silver, 2¾″ (7 cm) tall. Next is a simply cut cobalt blue overlay over clear with a silver neck and cap. On the end is a round bottle, deep green over clear, cut in a starburst pattern. Directly below this is a ruby overlay over clear, cut in a geometric pattern. Both are capped in silver. These five bottles are probably Bohemian, 1840–1880.

Three striped scent bottles in the second row of Fig. 3–10 are considered to be Venetian, c. 1820. The bottle on the left is pink, white, and clear, and the other two are blue, white, and clear. They are all cased over in clear glass. The second bottle from the right is cut and polished in simple flat planes on the front and sides. All are capped in brass.

The first bottle in the third row of Fig. 3–10 is deep ruby glass with panel-cut sides, simple cut shoulders, and a brass cap, c. 1850. Next is a blue bottle with hand-enameled flowers in orange, yellow, blue, white, and green. The cap is brass and has a tiny ring on either side to accommodate a ring chain. Next is a short cobalt bottle with simple panel cuts bearing minute amounts

Fig. 3–10

Left to right, top row: *Amethyst cut-to-clear with silver mount. Pink over white over clear cut in quatrefoil and trefoil designs, silver mount, 2¾" (7 cm) tall. Cobalt blue cut to clear silver mount. A green over clear with silver mount. Probably all are Bohemian, c. 1840. Center row: Pink, white, and clear. Cobalt blue, white, and clear. Dark blue, medium blue, white, and clear. All with brass mountings, probably Venetian, c. 1820. Ruby cut to clear, silver mount, probably Bohemian, c. 1850. Bottom row: Deep ruby glass, brass mount, mid-nineteenth century. Blue with enamel decoration, brass mount, German, c. 1875. Cobalt blue, panel cut, brass mount, early nineteenth century. Ruby glass, silver mount with carnelian set into cap, vinaigrette grid in neck, first half nineteenth century, probably Bohemian.*

of gold tracery. The cap is brass. These three are probably German in origin. The last bottle is truly rare. Of deep ruby glass with simple panel cuts, it has a mounting that makes it special. The silver is deeply cut in scroll designs, and set into the top in the center is a round, flat carnelian. The hinged cap opens to reveal a grille of silver cut into a very handsome rose with stem and leaves. This vinaigrette is possibly Bohemian or English and dates from the first half of the nineteenth century. See Figs. C-27 and C-28.

Double-Ended Scent Bottles

These came into general use about 1850, although a few were made in the late 1700s. They were highly popular until about 1875 but continued to be produced in smaller quantities until the end of the century. The double-ended bottles were made to serve a dual purpose, with smelling salts on one end and perfume on the other (Fig. 3–12). Usually the smelling salts end is easy to identify since many were made with a hinged, snap top. The cap snapped open when a small button on the neck was pressed. Inside the cap was a glass disk held in place with a strong spring to make a tight seal that kept the volatile fumes from escaping and corroding the metal mount. If a snap closure was not used, a tight-fitting, glass inner stopper was employed. Cork was used to keep the perfume end sealed, and often this side had cork embedded into the cap for this purpose.

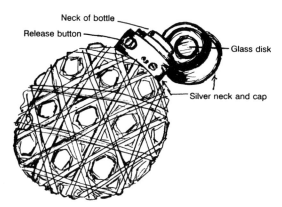

Fig. 3–11

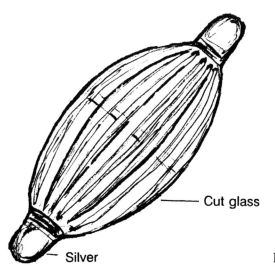

Fig. 3–12

Fig. 3–13

Double-ended scent bottles.

The five double-ended scent bottles in Fig. 3–13 are typical of the types manufactured during the second half of the nineteenth century.

At the far left is a small emerald green container with simple panel-cut sides and brass mounts. Next is a clear glass bottle, hand cut in the popular "Harvard" pattern, with silver mounts in fine repoussé. The next is ruby glass, which was the most frequently used color for double-ended scent bottles, with straight cut panels and mounts in sterling silver with a gold wash (silver gilt). One end unscrews and has a cork liner; the other end snaps open. The next bottle has clear glass cut in panels with silver gilt mounts. Inside the snap lid, impressed on a metal disk under the glass sealing disk, is "Mordan & Company, London." On the far right is a rare, apple green bottle, panel cut and unusually large, 6″ (15 cm) tall, with silver gilt mountings. Also impressed inside its snap lid is "Mordan & Co." Bottles in this photograph were probably all made in England. However, many double-ended scent bottles were made in Bohemia and elsewhere.

An unusual double-scent container, pictured in its case (Fig. 3–15), was made to fold in the center to take on the aspect of opera glasses. The mountings are solid gold, except for an area in the center that appears to be heavy silver gilt. The metal is hand-tooled with an emblem engraved in the top depicting Neptune nestled on a bed of ermine with trident and crown beside him. The bottle with the snap closure is still filled with cotton-wool with a rather unpleasant, lingering fragrance. The original case of brown sharkskin is lined in purple silk and velvet bearing the legend in gold, "D. C. Rait & Sons, Goldsmiths to the Queen." It was made in the second half of the nineteenth century. The box measures $3\frac{1}{2}″$ (9 cm) square.

Fig. 3–14

Left to right: *Deep ruby glass. Clear glass with ornate silver caps. Cobalt blue with fine silverwork. Clear glass with snap closure on one end. Ruby red bottle with snap closure for smelling salts on one end and vinaigrette on the other. All probably English, second half of the twentieth century. See also Fig. C-6.*

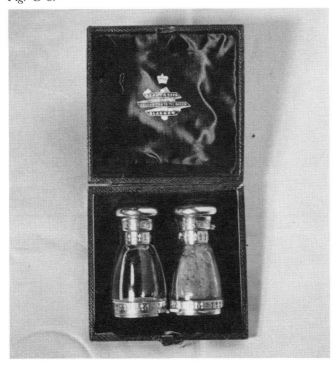

Fig. 3–15

Folding, double-scent bottles in case.

Lithyalin and Hyalith Glass

The first quarter of the nineteenth century was a time in which much experimentation took place in glassmaking. In Bohemia, Friedrich Egermann was trying to perfect glass that would resemble agate by using his "lithyalin" process. He succeeded in creating glass items in a variety of colors that closely resembled natural agate and patented the process in 1828. His innovation became so popular that glasshouses throughout Europe tried to simulate stone in glass. Baccarat of France produced a fine lithyalin-type glass that was used in their pressed "lacy" pieces.

Lithyalin bottles were made in various shapes and colors. A double-ended scent bottle, made in tans and browns, so closely resembled agate that it probably has fooled a great number of people in its many years of existence.

Meanwhile, a countryman of Egermann, George Franz August Longueval (Count von Buquoy), invented "hyalith," a black glass that some felt was inspired by Josiah Wedgwood's black basalt pottery. The glass was polished to a high sheen and was cut and decorated, usually in gold, in the popular chinoiserie style with insects and flowers. The cut was considered to be Oriental in fashion. If hyalith was produced with a matte finish, it took on the appearance of basalt ware.

The photograph of a scent bottle by Count von Buquoy in Fig. 3–17 clearly shows the angular cut, shape, flaring neck, and motif of gilded flowers and a butterfly. This is a typical example of the count's short-lived exploration of approximately ten years in the field of hyalith glass.

Fig. 3–16

Lithyalin bottle, sliver cap, $2\frac{1}{2}''$ (6.2 cm) tall.

Fig. 3–17
Hyalith bottle by Count von Buquoy, Bohemia, 3″ (7.5 cm) tall.

 # Dutch Scent Bottles

Bottles crafted by the Dutch are imaginative and graceful, but their excellent gold and silver work makes them particularly interesting. The glass can be in a variety of colors, but usually clear lead glass is seen with fine cutting. With the important China trade, the Dutch would mount gold or silver on dainty snuff bottles or other tiny porcelain bottles to create one-of-a-kind rarities. Delft pottery is often seen in large, heavy steins and chargers; however, even miniscule bottles were made, and these became charming scent holders.

The early Dutch bottles usually had cork stoppers with tiny silver pulls. Even those with solid gold caps were fitted with the cork stopper. Since the cork would dry up and crack apart, the original stopper is often missing. This should be of no concern to the buyer since tiny corks are easy to purchase if one feels it is necessary. If a glass stopper is in a bottle and it is from the eighteenth or early nineteenth century, it is probably a replacement.

One eighteenth century Dutch scent bottle was blown in a flat oval shape and bevel-cut around the sides (Fig. 3–18). On the front panel is an oval panel cut in tiny diamonds. The sides are wrapped in silver, scalloped, and hand decorated. The silver base is filled with a tarlike composition that surrounds an extension of the bottle, creating a solid foundation that enables it to stand. The neck and hinged cap are tooled. The bottle is $4\frac{1}{4}''$ high (10.5 cm) and marked with a Dutch silver hallmark.

Three excellent early bottles from the Netherlands shown in Fig. 3–21 illustrate the variety of scent bottles from that country. On the left is a tapered bottle in clear glass. It has cut panels halfway up, and each panel edge is cut in tiny notches. Above that, to the shoulder, are diamond cuts in rows, and from the shoulder to the neck are larger petal cuts. The spectacular mounting is solid gold, and minute, hand-engraved flowers are depicted in each tiny oval on the cap. Elsewhere are other floral designs and Dutch gold standard marks on both the neck and cap. The bottle is 4″ (10 cm) tall, c. 1800.

Fig. 3–18

Dutch scent bottle, c. 1780. Courtesy of and photograph by Fran Peters.

Fig. 3—19

A tiny Chinese blue and white porcelain vase is mounted by a nicely tooled solid gold cap with an inner stopper of gold and cork. About 3½" (9 cm), c. 1800. Dutch gold mark.

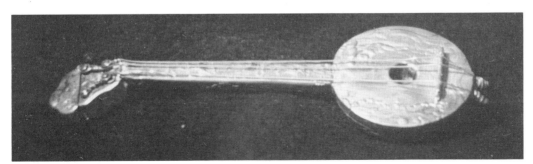

Fig. 3—20

Who would guess this little embossed silver mandolin hides a tiny scent bottle just above the frets? The very top lifts back on a hinge. It serves as a cover for the tiny bottle. Dutch, eighteenth century, 4¾" (11.5 cm) long.

Fig. 3–21

Dutch scent bottles, two in cut glass with solid gold mounts and one of delft pottery with silver mount. Photograph: Skylight Studio.

Fig. 3–22

A most unusual container for scent bottles in this minature drop-leaf table made of brass. A cage-work basket suspended under the table center holds four hand-blown bottles, each measuring $2\frac{1}{2}$" (6 cm) high and $1\frac{3}{8}$" (3.5 cm) square. Cap, neck, and shoulder mounts are finely embossed brass bearing traces of gold. The table measures $9\frac{1}{2}$" (24 cm) by 8" (20 cm) when extended. Drop leaves, hinged and supported by wire braces, have reverse paintings on glass that exquisitely illustrate famous Paris landmarks, such as Notre Dame and the Madeleine. Mother-of-pearl backing the paintings imparts a lively glow. Two larger pictures on top measure $2\frac{1}{2}$" (7 cm) by 2" and depict the newly finished Arc de Triomphe and the Pantheon. These two pictures are hinged and lift to reveal the four scent bottles. All pictures are set in narrow brass frames. The surrounding brass areas are decorated with hand-tooled floral designs, with a thin framework around the table edge tooled in a Greek key design. The table is $4\frac{1}{4}$" (10.5 cm) tall. French origin, c. 1836.

The unique, tiny bottle at the center in Fig. 3–21 is a masterpiece. This wee ewer in delft pottery has a portrait of a man on each side. Leafy scrolls decorate the rest of the container. Its cork stopper is attached to a silver mount that is secured to the bottle handle by a dainty silver chain. At right in the photograph is a simple, panel-cut bottle with a round foot, c. 1800. The solid gold mounting extending from the neck and partly down the bottle makes it truly outstanding. Its hinged cap is enhanced with repoussé. The gold standard mark is incised in the cap and neck.

Fig. 3–23

Most unusual set of four opalene bottles (two blue, two green) with tooled gilded brass work. The stand is ornate gilded brass with four round medallions in porcelain delicately painted with flowers. Three of the bottles have like medallions inserted in the tops and one has a tiny plaque in bronze commemorating a Bryn Mawr horse show for which it was given as a prize. The base is white marble. The bottles are about 4½″ (11 cm) high. French, third quarter nineteenth century. (See Fig. C-33).

Fig. 3–24

Cobalt blue is a favorite color among collectors. The rich, deep hue seems to be enhanced by cutting. This example is topped by an intricate, hand-tooled silver mounting, c. 1850, mid-European, 3⅝″ (9 cm) tall.

Fig. 3-25

This elegant cobalt blue bottle cased in clear glass was cut in flat planes, tapering from neck to shoulder, and mounted with vermeil machined in a tiny diamond pattern. It bears the 1838 French silver standard mark. Height, 4¼" (10.5 cm).

Fig. 3-26

Very tall double-overlay scent bottle is deep cobalt blue over white, cut through to clear, with high-waisted shape emphasized by cutting. A superb, hand-chased, heavy silver cap crowns this beauty. Origin probably mid-European, c. 1850.

Fig. 3–27

This scent bottle in clear apple green is deeply cut, very heavy, and blown from lead glass with uranium added to achieve the fine coloring. The silver cap was intricately hand tooled in a floral and scroll motif. Probably Bohemian origin, c. 1875, it is 4½" (10.5 cm) tall.

Fig. 3–28

Clear cut glass over deep red, hand enameled, and trimmed in gold. European, probably Bohemian, c. 1830, 3" (7.5 cm).

Fig. 3-29

Elegant lead glass bottle, simply cut. Glass cap and bottle are joined by a silver-plated metal collar, 5″ long (12.6 cm).

Fig. 3-30

Baroque in style, this little scent bottle is in ornate silver with two seraphim on the shoulders and stoppered by a cork attached to a silver rabbit finial. Eighteenth-century European.

4

Early American Perfume and Scent Bottles

Early American glass holds a special fascination for collectors, but the excitement that comes with finding the rarities created by our forefathers is more than patriotic fervor. The early glass possesses a simplicity and honesty of line that makes it very appealing.

Because America was a colony of England and not allowed to blow glass in the Colonial period, glasshouses were not developed until the United States had achieved independence. In scent bottles as in tableware, glass in Colonial America was of British and European origin. After the Revolutionary War, the elegance created for an aristocracy was little needed in the struggling new country. American glass manufacturing was for the most part utilitarian until the middle of the nineteenth century.

The earliest glassblowers in America to make a name for themselves were German immigrants. Wistar (who was producing glass in defiance of the British), Stiegel and Amelung started blowing simple glass for day-to-day use. Some of the fancier glass from this period was blown in colors and decorated with enameling or engraving, but usually the work was quite primitive. Early American glass demonstrated a strong German influence due to the national origin of the three men who started these glasshouses.

Early scent bottles were free blown and in whimsical shapes, such as the sea horse scent bottles in Fig. 4–2, which were made by drawing out a long tube of glass and deftly winding the end into a tight coil. Sometimes rigaree and quilling were quickly applied as decoration, or canes of colored glass might be used to give extra interest to the bottle (Fig. C-17).

Three fine examples of Early American scent bottles dating from about 1800 are shown in Fig. C-53. The deep amber-colored glass is a free-blown bottle with quilling applied continuously around the sides. The waisted bottle has an indentation on the front and back. In the center is a sea horse scent bottle in extremely rare amethyst and white stripes, decorated in ribbonlike quilling and rigaree. At right is a simple hand-blown and tooled cobalt blue scent bottle known as the "Stiegel type."

Three bottles from the late 1700s display techniques of applied decoration (Fig. 4–2). All are in clear glass, although the sea horse scent bottle on the right has opaque white canes to add interest. Each would have been corked. The bottle on the left is 4″ (10 cm) long.

By 1820, many glasshouses existed in the United States along the East Coast, in Pennsylvania, and in Ohio. Some of the famous glass companies founded at this time were the New England Glass Company, the Boston and Sandwich Glass Company, and the Bakewell Glass Company of Pittsburgh. They all produced free-blown, blown-through-mold, pressed glass, and cut glass. Soon their fine, innovative glass was rivaling imports from Europe (Figs. 4–5 and C-14).

Showing the development of American bottles from the time of the Revolution to the Civil War are five bottles shown in Fig. 4–6. Two sea horse

Fig. 4–1

Three early bottles. On the left is a shield shape with beaded edges and sunburst center, mold blown, clear glass. New England area, c. 1825, 3″ (7.6 cm) tall. Also from the same era is a finely cut bottle in aqua glass that is collared in silver and has a simple ground stopper of the same color. On the right is a mold-blown bottle in pale aqua depicting the gothic arch theme with a figure described as a Hessian soldier. This bottle and that on the left would have had cork stoppers.

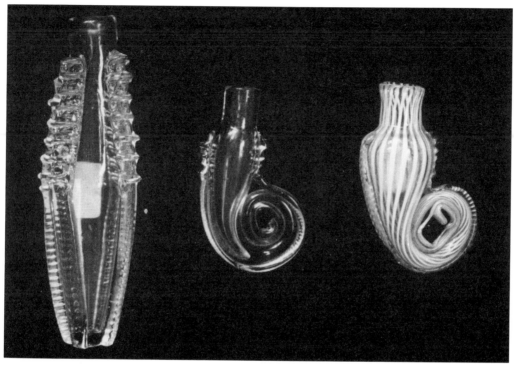

Fig. 4–2

Left and center: *American clear glass scents with applied decoration, quilling, and tooling.* Right: *Sea horse scent with opaque white stripes in clear glass, applied tooled strips, and rigaree. All date from the late 1700s through 1820.*

Fig. 4–3

Left to right: *Three early blown-in-the-mold scent bottles. Aqua lyre-shaped bottle. Variation of lyre shape, about 4½″ (11.5 cm) tall. Fountain bottle, 1825–1840, probably American.* Courtesy of Fran Peters.

scent bottles, one with cobalt stripes and one clear, are the earliest (1790–1820). A rare, blown-in-the-mold, lyre-shaped bottle with a copper screw-on cap bearing traces of silver dates c. 1825. Next to it is a mold-blown, pale aqua cologne bottle in lyre shape, also c. 1825. It would have been corked. On the far right is an amethyst-colored smelling salts bottle in pressed glass

Fig. 4–4

Three mold-blown cologne bottles dating from the mid-nineteenth century. Left to right: Amethyst-colored bottle, 3½" (9 cm) tall. Pale aquamarine-colored bottle with floral bouquet design. Gothic arch-shaped bottle in medium blue. Courtesy of Fran Peters.

Fig. 4–5

On the left is an American mold-blown bottle with "MORRIS JOHNSON N-YORK" impressed above the columns. The bottle is exactly like one made in France similar to the Pantheon except for the inscription. On the right is a pressed flint bottle made by the Sandwich Glass Company in the mid-nineteenth century in the star and punty design. A garland has been engraved onto the shoulder and stopper; 6" (15 cm) tall.

with a pewter cap in an embossed rose motif. This is attributed to Boston and Sandwich, c. 1850, and measures 3" (7.5 cm) tall.

A handsome cologne bottle from Boston and Sandwich, pressed in amber flint glass (early lead glass is usually called "flint") and decorated by hand in gold flowers was made around 1840 and is 5" (12.5 cm) tall (Fig. 4–7). Collectors seek Boston and Sandwich glass avidly. Colored pieces are especially treasured because the glass has great clarity and the colors are brilliant.

The study of American glass can be very rewarding. There are wonderful books on the subject and many museums where fine examples can be seen. Some of these are listed in the Bibliography and Museums sections of this

Fig. 4–6

Left to right: *Two sea horse scent bottles, one in amethyst and white stripes with clear glass rigaree and quilling and the other in clear glass, with similar decoration. Mold-blown, lyre-shaped bottle with copper cap. Lyre-shaped cologne, mold blown in pale aquamarine. Smelling salts bottle pressed in amethyst-colored glass with embossed pewter cap by Boston and Sandwich, c. 1850. All American-made.*

Fig. 4–7

Pressed-glass cologne bottle in amber flint glass hand trimmed in gold. Probably by the Boston and Sandwich Glass Company or made by Baccarat and decorated by Boston and Sandwich, c. 1840. Courtesy of Fran Peters.

book. Learning to recognize colors, shapes, and quality will take devotion and a lot of time, but the experience can be very enriching.

Other Early American scent bottles were made of stone, silver, and various metals. Only the Tucker Company made porcelain during this period, and probably very few, if any, scent bottles were produced by them.

5

Chatelaines

Another field of interest for the perfume and scent bottle collector, and a challenge to find, are chatelaines. Chatelaines came in a great variety of shapes, materials, and sizes. They were made for a multitude of uses but mainly served as decorative accessories worn by ladies.

The word "chatelaine" originated in medieval times when the men of the great castles carried keys to the numerous rooms on chains hanging from their belts. While they were away fighting in the Crusades, they entrusted the keys to their ladies and left them in charge of the castle. The ladies became known as *castellans,* or chatelaines.

During Victorian times, chatelaines were adapted as popular items of jewelry. From a hook or clasp that fastened to the belt, chains, usually one to five, were suspended that carried a wide variety of objects. The selection seemed to be limited only by the jeweler's or metalsmith's imagination.

Sewing chatelaines were crafted that held scissors, a needle case, thimble, measuring tape, or other accoutrements. Chatelaines for evening wear might consist of a scent bottle, a dance program with ivory leaves in a silver, mother-of-pearl, or tortoiseshell case, a pencil for marking the partners of each dance, and a tiny mesh purse.

To think of anyone dancing with those clanking and banging encumbrances seems strange to twentieth century minds, but Victorians loved their fancy trappings and decorated their persons as ornately as they furnished their homes.

It is rare to see a complete chatelaine now. Many times various pieces have been removed and sold, lost, or damaged.

A very fine example of a chatelaine in sterling silver from the 1880s is shown in Fig. 5–1. The ornate belt piece, backed with a hinged belt hook, depicts what is probably the Virgin Mary seated with the Infant Jesus held in one arm and John the Baptist standing at her right. A filigree halo radiates around her head, and five repoussé-linked chains descend from the centerpiece. On the back of the hook is the jeweler's mark, impressed with a crown, "James Atchison, 60 Princes St., Edinburgh." It also bears London 1889–1890 hallmarks, plus the initials of the silversmith, W. Comyns. All swivels are marked with London hallmarks.

On the chain to the farthest left is a whistle, with London hallmarks. Next is a fine scent bottle, and the marks are the silversmith's initials, probably Scottish. In the center is a most interesting piece that combines not only a penknife blade but a tiny pair of scissors and a miniature corkscrew for removing the corks from scent bottles. There is no mark on the silver knife. At center right is a pencil holder marked "S. Mordan & Co." (Located in London, Mordan was a prolific maker of scent bottles, jewelry, and allied objects in the second half of the nineteenth century.) On the far right is a pair of scissors encased in a velvet-lined sheath and marked on one blade, "Encore." The

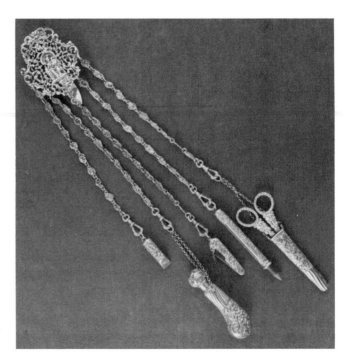

Fig. 5–1

Silver chatelaine of English craft-manship from a private collection.

scissors and sheath are 5″ (12.5 cm) long. The entire chatelaine measures about 16″ (35 cm) in length.

Queen Victoria, sovereign of the British Empire for many years, presided over many changes during her reign. One of them involved the traditional mourning costume. When her beloved consort, Prince Albert, died, Queen Victoria adopted black mourning garb and wore it until her death. With the queen setting the trend in bereavement fashions, the world quickly fell into step, and black mourning jewelry became an important part of the proper mourning costume.

Perfume and scent bottles were also designed as suitable accessories to be worn during the mourning period. A fine example is this black jet scent bottle cut in tapered urn style and geometric in design (Fig. 5–2). It has a matching cap pierced with holes in the top to allow the bearer to sniff the contents without removing the cap. A chain, cleverly carved from one piece of jet, is fastened to side handles on the bottle and attached to a large ring that suspends from the reticulated, triangular belt piece. The belt piece conceals a hook that

Fig. 5–2

Victorian-era mourning chatelaines. Carved jet on left and black amethyst glass with silver-plated metal at right are from private collections. Photograph: Skylight Studio.

could be slipped over a belt or waistband. At the top of the belt piece is a beautifully carved head of a woman wearing a medieval headdress and a double strand of beads. The entire chatelaine is 9″ (22.5 cm) long. It was made in the middle 1800s.

Also shown in Fig. 5–2 is a chatelaine that also could have been worn during mourning. The bottle of black amethyst glass is cut in flat triangles, mounted in delicate metalwork that is plated in silver. The hinged cap is openwork, and a tiny ground stopper seals the contents. The chain is suspended from a belt piece that has a large black amethyst "jewel" and a hook on the right side. Perhaps this hook was to hold a lorgnette on a chain. Made in the second half of the nineteenth century, this chatelaine measures 7½″ (19 cm) long.

A chatelaine could be simple or very extravagant. One that must have caused much comment was made of solid silver, tooled and enameled in white (see Fig. C-36). Both the flask-shaped bottle and the round frontal plate of the hook were mounted with turquoise and garnets. It was hallmarked proving it to be from the Austro-Hungarian area of Europe and made somewhere around 1840 or 1850. The brown leather presentation box was made just to fit the chatelaine and was lined in a fine red velvet. A very unusual feature was the addition of a tiny pin, rather the forerunner of the present-day safety pin, attached to the chatelaine by a fine silver chain.

6

Infinite Varieties

Probably the most exciting part of pursuing an interest in perfume and scent bottles is the fantastic diversity of the containers. Just when it seems there could not be another way to package or apply the scents, another variation pops up.

Sometimes the bottle is whimsically shaped or made from an unusual material. Sometimes the way it was used is even more fascinating.

Precious and semiprecious stones have been chosen to decorate scent containers throughout the ages, but, due to the difficulty of finding and carving a stone without cracks and faults large enough for the purpose, they were seldom made into bottles. Probably the earliest stone bottles were of alabaster, which is easily carved. However, alabaster has a porous quality and is not the best material to house and protect delicate substances from air and spoilage.

Agate, jasper, quartz, bloodstone, granite, opal, topaz, malachite, and other stones have been used to create more satisfactory containers. All are considered rare, and the more precious the stone, the more expensive the bottle.

Bottles were occasionally made from rock crystal. To cut into hard quartz and create a bottle must have been quite a feat, particularly before the advent of power tools. These bottles were expensive to make considering the time and effort expended; add to that the cutting, grinding, and polishing required to finish it, the silver or gold mounting, and the adding of precious stones and the cost must have been astronomical. See Fig. C-30.

When an especially wonderful bottle is discovered, curiosity about its history seems to fire the imagination. One special bottle is cylinder shaped, cut from rock crystal with the exterior covered in tiny, shallow, circular cuts (See Color Fig. C-30). It was made in Russia in the nineteenth century. The neck and cap were encased in heavy gold foil inside and out, then countless cut garnets were mounted to cover most of the gold. The French influence can be clearly seen in the design. It would be fascinating to know the history of this bottle.

In the late 1600s, George Ravenscroft of England added lead to glass, and this brilliant, less-brittle glass allowed glassmakers a new medium with which to work. It not only sparkled and rang like a bell but it cut easier.

In the eighteenth century, the French were particularly fond of disguising bottle sets in leather cases that looked like a book when closed. The cases were so cleverly made with gold tooling and lettering decorating the leather that only a very sharp eye could detect the deception.

Often two tiny scent bottles, usually very plainly cut, would nestle in separate compartments in the cases. The "books" opened at their middles to reveal compartmented bottles on the left and right. The bottles were usually topped by simple silver or gold caps or by corks with gold fittings that were attached to the collar ring by minute chains.

Another interesting bottle, cut in a plain square shape that tapers slightly toward the neck, is from a bloodstone (Fig. 6–1). The base, neck, and cap are of silver enameled in white and red. The Roman numeral VIII repeats around the base. It is of Russian or Greek origin, late eighteenth or early nineteenth century, and 2½″ (6 cm) tall.

Metal-mounted scent bottles were very popular in Europe. Opaline bottles were often suspended in fancy brass wire stands. Animals, such as bronze goats or horses, created in perfect detail drew tiny carts or other vehicles with a scent bottle as the precious burden. (See Figs. C-26 and C-29.)

Bottles have been produced in the shapes of binoculars, umbrellas, birds, animals, and kerosene lamps. Per-

Fig. 6–1

Bloodstone scent bottle.

Fig. 6–2

A charming figurine of a pretty lady was molded in metal and enameled in bright colors. She carries a basket woven of bronze wires that contains two little clear glass scent bottles with facet-cut stoppers. In the other hand, she carries a parasol of pink silk that really is a pincushion stuffed with sawdust. European, second half of the nineteenth century, about 5½" (14 cm) tall.

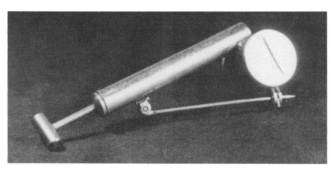

Fig. 6–3

Flit gun, 2" (5 cm) long. Courtesy of and photograph by Fran Peters.

fume bottles and scent containers were made in the form of rings, necklaces, musical instruments, and novelty items, such as the unusual "atomizer" pictured here.

From the 1930s in America came the "flit gun" or fly sprayer perfume. It was a tiny replica of a commercially produced household sprayer (Fig. 6–3). This example was adapted to use as a pin. To fill, the drum could be opened on one end by unscrewing the cover. The perfume sprayed out when the handle on the pressure tube was pumped. Usually the flit gun came without a pin and could be carried in a purse or placed on a dresser.

Another way of applying perfume was by use of the sprinkler cap. The metal stopper, usually shaped like a rose or daisy, was made with holes in the top. When it was screwed open, the perfume could be shaken out a few drops at a time. Bottles of this type date from the twentieth century.

The important porcelain manufacturers of Europe all produced perfume containers of various shapes and sizes.

In England, there were many fine porcelain manufacturers. One of these was at Coalport, where they designed bottles and decorated them with hand-painted miniature scenes or creative enamel glazes. They used tiny colored, raised dots of enamel to give the appearance of jewels, then gold was applied in lavish proportion. Sometimes the bottles had porcelain stoppers and others were delightfully capped with silver gilt (Fig. C-13).

Additional famous companies were, of course, Chelsea, with the "Girl on a Swing" figural scent bottles of the eighteenth century, along with Derby, Minton, and others.

Even double-ended bottles were made from porcelain, but these are very rare. One is illustrated in Fig. C-6.

The Royal Worchester factory manufactured many lovely scent bottles, some resembling shields, some ribbed, and some hand painted with delicate flowers or realistic birds against an ivory-colored background. Most were marked on the back with the gold insignia of Royal Worchester. (See Fig. C-41.)

The dog with a clown collar and hat in Fig. 6–4 is not a very sophisticated figural example. In grayish pressed glass, it appears to be American, c. 1890.

In 1925, the Philadelphia Sesquicentennial was celebrated and the Liberty Bell was replicated in the form of a pressed glass perfume bottle at that time (Fig. 6–5). On one side is the following: "F. HOYT & Co., CELEBRATED PERFUMERS, ESTB 1869." On the other side are the years, "1715–1925." The stopper is obviously a replacement. It was probably stoppered with a cork originally.

In the mid-twentieth century, the ballpoint applicator came on the scene. A metal container unscrewed in the middle to reveal cotton that could be saturated with perfume. When the pieces were rejoined, the user could roll the scent on with the revolving applicator on the top.

Fig. 6–4

Clown dog bottle. Courtesy of and photograph by Fran Peters.

Fig. 6–5

Libery Bell perfume bottle with replacement stopper. Courtesy of and photograph by Fran Peters.

Throwaway Scent Bottles

Among the lay-down scent bottles of the late eighteenth and nineteenth centuries are the "throwaway" or "Attar of Rose" bottles. These long, narrow bottles, made to hold only a few drops of scent, were sold at spas, fairs, and shops and were not made to refill.

The majority of these bottles were made in Germanic areas of Europe, more for the common people than the wealthier classes. Throwaway scent bottles waned in popularity toward the end of the nineteenth century. Most measured 7″ to 8″ in length, which included a ground stopper with a round flat top. Throwaways were usually made of clear glass, but occasionally bottles in blue, green, amber, or other colors are found. They were hand-blown and hand-decorated with ovals, crisscrosses, flat planes, and spirals cut into the glass. Enamels and a lot of gold were applied, and, occasionally, examples are seen that were exquisitely made. In general, they were rather crude.

Shown in Fig. 6–6 are two specimens. On the left is a deep blue bottle with sides and bottom cut in flat panels. Gold decoration is laid on in interlacing scallops and a leaf motif decorates the sides. Red and green "jewels" make this a little fancier than the usual lavender. This one might have been made on the Continent. The bottle on the right is typical of the kind of throwaway scent bottle that can be found today. Made of clear glass, it is roughly cut in crisscrosses and ovals and decorated in gold.

Perhaps this is a good time to try to put a popular misconception to rest. These lavender bottles, sometime or somehow, became labeled by someone as "tear bottles." This romantic name, sentimental and appealing as it might be, is simply not appropriate. These bottles were not made to hold tears.

Legends about "tear bottles" are always romantic. Some storytellers cite ancient Egypt, Rome, or China as the land of origin. Others claim that during

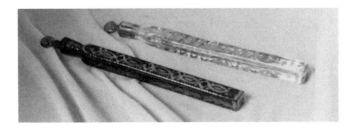

Fig. 6–6

Throwaway scent bottles.

Fig. C-25 *A bottle of clear glass with ruby flashing cut to clear. Roundels on the sides are delicately engraved with flowers. A superb example of the cutting done in Bohemia during the third quarter of the nineteenth century; about $6\frac{1}{2}''$ (16cm) tall.*

Fig. C-26

Fig. C-27

Fig. C-28

Fig. C-26 *A single bronze goat with detailed harness draws a ring that is the holder for an aqua-colored bottle blown, cut, and enameled. Probably French, 1850–1875.*

Fig. C-27 *Four scent bottles in a variety of greens. Left to right: A clear apple-green bottle, nicely cut and topped with an ornate silver mount. A cut uranium glass, waisted bottle with a pretty silver mount. Opalene apple-green scent with brass screw-on cap. A deep green overlay cut to clear, about 3½" (9cm) tall. All European, nineteenth century.*

Fig. C-28 *Three bottles, cut from a colored layer to clear. Left to right: A most unusual "smelling" bottle; cobalt blue over clear, topped off with a hinged flat lid that merely rests instead of creating a tight seal; the bottle contains cotton and was evidently soaked in scent and merely inhaled by the user; England, late nineteenth century. A beautifully cut bottle with just a hint of the red overlay left; the finely embossed silver-hinged lid snaps open when the button is pushed. English, 1850 to 1875, 3¾" (9.5cm) tall. Blue over clear bottle, very nicely cut and mounted in silver; probably European, c. 1875.*

Fig. C-29 *Green opalene scent bottle rests in a brass stand; French, c. 1880.*

Fig. C-29

Fig. C-32

Fig. C-30

Fig. C-30 *An extraordinary Russian bottle of quartz crystal cut in tiny, shallow, roundish cuts. The metal mounting is encased inside and out in heavy gold foil. Intricate fleur-de-lis were applied over the foil on the tops and sides, and myriad garnets were cut and individually mounted. A large cabochon garnet graces the top, and smaller ones are mounted on the sides. Marked in Cyrillic letters; second half of the nineteenth century; $2\frac{3}{4}''$ (7cm) tall.*

Fig. C-31 *Triple layers of glass, deep blue over white cut to clear, decorated with gold. The cap is most unusual in that it is an ivory fruit basket expertly carved in delicate detail. European, c. 1830; about $4\frac{1}{2}''$ (11.5cm) tall.*

Fig. C-32 *Very Victorian is this wonderful red plush box. The sides and front are inset with cut glass panes. The front lifts up and folds back to reveal two square-cut bottles. A silken pink rose was appliquéd inside the lid. Probably American, c. 1880; about 8" (20cm) tall.*

Fig. C-31

Fig. C-33

Fig. C-34

Fig. C-33 *Green and blue bottles in an ornate brass stand (see Chapter 3, "The Fabulous French," for description).*

Fig. C-34 *Wonderful satyr's-head bottle by Thomas Webb in ivory glass with brown staining; original silver-gilt mount; lush presentation case, c. 1885; 6" (13cm) long.*

Fig. C-37

Fig. C-35

Fig. C-36

Fig. C-35 *Three porcelain bottles in the shape of umbrellas—with handles as stoppers—rest in a gilded brass stand with a finial and base of porcelain. All are hand enameled and gold trimmed, c. 1875, probably Dresden; about 10″ (25cm) tall.*

Fig. C-36 *From the Austria-Hungarian region came this chatelaine made of silver, tooled and enameled. Both the large circular piece to which the hook was attached and the bottle were lavishly set with fine turquoise and garnets. Both sides of the bottle were jeweled. Silver chains connected the two pieces, and a delicate "safety pin" was suspended to provide extra security. The chatelaine came in its original leather box; mid-nineteenth century; about 4½″ (11cm) long.*

Fig. C-37 *An excellent example of English cameo is this bottle of white cut to a silky red glass. The cap is a simple screw-on in silver gilt. The 4½″ (11cm) bottle comes in its own velvet- and silk-lined leather presentation case.*

Fig. C-38

Fig. C-39

Fig. C-38 *A set of tiny French sample perfumes in a pretty gift box, c. 1950.*

Fig. C-39 *Four Mary Chess perfumes in their colorful presentation box. All are shaped like chess pieces. New York, 1930s and 1940s. The bottles are 3" (7.5cm) high.*

Fig. C-40 *At left is a perfume by Lubin in a classic bottle and original box. At right is a set of three perfumes by Lanvin in a fitted box with silk lining. Both from the 1930s.*

Fig. C-40

Fig. C-41

Fig. C-42

Fig. C-43

Fig. C-41 *A shield-shaped porcelain bottle with a gold Royal Worcester mark, c. 1875. Finely hand-painted bird on a branch in yellow, red, browns, and gold; 3½" (8.5 cm) high.*

Fig. C-42 *Victorian perfume holder made of brass and brass wire has a heart-shaped beveled mirror and a pin tray mounted between the two pressed-glass bottles, 5" (12.5cm), which are hand painted. Fourth quarter of the nineteenth century.*

Fig. C-43 *A clear glass bottle is housed in a green box that opens by use of silken cords with tiny weights. Russian, mid-twentieth century.*

Fig. C-44 *Three scent bottles from England, late eighteenth century. Left to right: Wedgwood jasperware bottle in extremely rare moss-green with silver stopper. Rare tricolor Wedgwood, moss-green with blue medallion in the center and white trim; cap is carved ivory. Jasperware bottle made by John Turner.*

Fig. C-44

Fig. C-45

Fig. C-45 Upper left: *Agate scent bottle carved in simple panels with agate stopper. Filigreed sterling silver mounting with gold wash. Amethyst-colored cabochon at crest. Probably American, second half nineteenth century, 4" (10cm) long.* Upper right: *Banded agate scent bottle with mounting of solid gold, handtooled in scrolled leaf design. Hinged cap reveals engraved "July 22, 1843"; American, 1¾" (4cm) long. Private collection.* Lower left: *Rare tortoiseshell bottle. Piqué of pure gold stars embedded in surface; sides of bottle joined by thin strip of vermeil; upper portion encased in vermeil cutwork; vermeil cap hand engraved. On the back is a tiny shield of solid gold engraved with two Es in fancy script. Marked "Paris 1838"; 4½" (9cm) high. Private collection.* Lower center: *Mother-of-pearl bottle with silver-plated metal frame; unusual neck detail; metal cap with mother-of-pearl inset. Unknown maker, last half of nineteenth century.* Lower right: *Made to be worn to a Viennese ball, with emblem of men's guild sponsor Kaufmannschen Vereines, mounted on front panel. Winged staff, sides, cap, and pedestal foot are ormolu; shield is enamel over metal; foot and neckpiece have precious, semiprecious, and imitation jewels, some set into ormolu and some in deep collars, Holbien style. Catch releases a hinged panel, exposing a printed dance program, dated February 10, 1885. Private collection. Photograph: Skylight Studio.*

the Crusades (the most popular era for the tear bottle fable) while knights were off fighting the Saracens, their pining ladies saved their tears to show how much they grieved for their men during their absence. One person even referred to a scent bottle of a different shape as a "lacrymal vessel," which probably elevated it a step above the so-called tear bottle. It would have been difficult to cry into the tiny openings these bottles provided, but perhaps ladies of long ago carried funnels on their chatelaines for that purpose.

For some reason or other, these bottles have been such a subject of conjecture over the years that numerous other names have been given to them; unfortunately, the imaginative stories that were accorded them seem to have lived on. They are not boot bottles, lapel bottles, or bosom bottles.

A bottle of similar shape, but usually found in pressed glass, held "Otto of Roses," a very popular scent from the mid-1800s to the early 1900s. The c. 1900 bottle in Fig. 6–7 has a tiny diamond motif and a cut glass stopper. It rests on its original box and measures 5½" (14 cm) long.

Fig. 6–7

Otto of Roses perfume. Courtesy of and photograph by Fran Peters.

Fig. 6–8

Porcelain perfume bottles from the first quarter of the twentieth century, in apple green glaze with black lines accenting the necks. Both have cork stoppers, glass droppers. The larger is marked "Germany" on the base and is 5¾" (15 cm) tall. The smaller one is marked "Bavaria."

Fig. 6–9

Flat oval bottle with sides cut in shallow diamonds has a fine engraving on the front depicting a stag. Cap in silver plate was probably engraved by an artist of the German tradition, either in Europe or the United States, c. 1860, 3¼" (8 cm) long.

Fig. 6–10

Horn-shaped bottles from the late 1800s were and are very popular. This deep sky blue one has white daisies with gold centers painted on it. Others made in clear glass shading to blue, green, and other colors were given an acid bath, as this one was, to produce a satin finish that was enameled with white flowers. They are set with silver caps, sometimes marked "sterling," and some bear English hallmarks. They must have been popular in both countries. Length, 3¾" (9.5 cm).

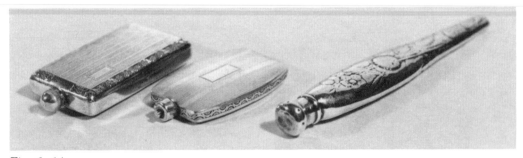

Fig. 6–11

These sterling silver containers were American-made. Left: Rectangular purse perfume with screw top, tailored stripe design, and floral edge. Impressed into the bottom, "Pat. 6–22–26." Center: A similar piece with tapered body, push-button applicator in the cap, also from the 1920s. Right: Glove perfumer, hand chased with various types of flowers. The cap has perforations in the top that release scent when it is unscrewed slightly, c. 1880.

Fig. 6–12

Left: Metal snowman with silver-colored top and a golden bottom conceals a round bottle containing My Love perfume by Elizabeth Arden, identified by a label on the base. Height, 1⅝″ (5 cm). Right: Purse perfumer encased in green and white streaked celluloid with chromed metal. Small button at top of base depresses to release perfume drop. It fills from the bottom. Probably American, 2¼″ (5.5 cm) tall. Both bottles c. 1925.

Fig. 6–13

A white blown opaline glass bottle and stopper is decorated with red and green "jewels" and gold tracery. Probably French, late nineteenth century. Height, 5″ (12.5 cm).

Fig. 6–14

Left: *An exquisite, hand-painted portrayal of Achilles, Ulysses, and Thebes, accented with yellow and gold motif, graces this porcelain bottle with silver neck chain and cap. Royal Vienna blue beehive mark, from last half of nineteenth century. Height, 3″ (7.5 cm). Center: Porcelain figural bottle of a whippet. Head forms the stopper, and collar and inner neckpiece are gold plated. Probably German, nineteenth century, 5½″ (14.5 cm) long. Private collection. Right: Baby wrapped in white bunting with black dots, magenta ribbons, and bows. Hinged opening at bottom is rimmed in gilded metal. Early nineteenth century, possibly German.*

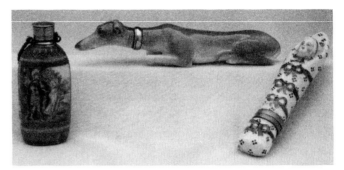

Smelling Salts

7

At one time, spirits of ammonia was considered to be a necessity of everyday life and was carried by both men and women. Vials were hastily employed when a lady suffered from an attack of the "vapors."

In 1884, a two-volume set of books was published with the title *Encyclopedia of Health and Home (A Domestic Guide to Health, Wealth, and Happiness, Thorough and Exhaustive and Adapted to the Easy Apprehension of All Classes)*. A chapter in Volume II discussing spirits of ammonia, aqua ammonia, and spirits of hartshorn described their use:

> *It is employed in hooping-cough, delirium tremens, and in prostration from exhausting discharges, as a stimulant, as an antacid in heartburn, acid stomach, and sick headache caused by acid stomach; and applied to the nostrils as a stimulant in fainting, headache, etc. . . . It should not be used internally, except when largely diluted with water, otherwise it will act as a corrosive poison. . . . When ammonia is combined with sweet oil it makes a good liniment.*

Spirits of ammonia could be used in many ways, but as a smelling salts it was a popular favorite. Why were so many women fainting or otherwise claiming a need for smelling salts? Certainly, for some, it was a feminine device. However, many were in genuine need of the restorative powers of smelling salts because of their fashionably restrictive clothing.

The tight lacing of milady's middle was important from the Renaissance until the early twentieth century. Remember *Gone With the Wind*, when Scarlett urged Mammy to pull the laces tighter, and Mammy, in her comfortable and well-filled-out calico, chided Scarlett for eating like a field hand? Fashion then decreed a 20″ or smaller waistline. Corsets to create this appearance were instruments of torture that could injure or even kill the women wearing them. Stomachs were squashed and ribs restrained or broken, but even on the hottest summer days, corsets, covered with layers and layers of petticoats, were worn.

To quote the *Encyclopedia of Health and Home* again, "Only the anatomist knows the frightful misplacement of the internal organs of the body that is caused by the suicidal habit of tight lacing. It gives rise more or less to that depression of spirits so common to young ladies; and worse still, occasionally originates or aggravates organic disease of the most serious description."

Usually smelling salts came from the apothecary or druggist in rather mundane bottles. They were meant to be decanted into something nicer to carry. An exception is a flat, round, deep green bottle with a glass stopper in the shape of a crown. The label identifies it as a product of the Crown Perfumery Company, London, England. Not only is the bottle attractive, it even has its own kid leather snap purse. Made about 1900, it is 3½″ (9 cm) tall. (See Fig. C-49.)

Because ammonia can etch the glass of a bottle when left in it for a time, some bottles will take on a cloudy appearance that is referred to as "sick glass." With double-ended scent bottles, it is often easy to pick out the end that contained the salts because of the presence of this etching.

Fig. 7–1

Smelling salts bottle by the Sandwich Glass Company, Sandwich, Massachusetts, has its original pewter cap. Deep amethyst color appears black until viewed under strong light. It was pressed in a mold and has a threaded neck. Made c. 1850, it is 2⅜″ (6 cm) high.

8

Cameo Glass

The technique of casing one layer of glass over another and cutting through the layers to decorate the glass was invented about two thousand years ago. The most celebrated piece of cameo glass is the Portland vase made by the Romans in the first century A.D. It was mold blown, white-over-black, and the cameo-cut motif depicted the Roman gods.

For centuries, the Chinese also produced fine layered glass carved in patterns featuring natural, religious, and mythical subjects.

In the Western world, a great surge of interest in the art of cameo glass occured in the last half of the nineteenth century. France and England led the field in experimentation, new techniques, and production.

English Cameo Glass

The great glasshouses of England were Stevens and Williams, Thomas Webb and Sons, the Richardsons, and others. Cameo glasss scent bottles were made in a variety of shapes and sizes. Sometimes three layers of glass would be used, but more often two colors produced the desired results (Fig. C-37).

Shown in Fig. 8–1 and also in Fig. C-64, are five excellent examples of cameo glass scent bottles. At the top left is a round, slightly flattened bottle in opaque off-white, cased in a thin layer of deep pink and an outer layer of pale pink. The layers were cut into a morning glory and vine design, with the undulating lines recalling the soft, flowing curves of the Art Nouveau move-

Fig. 8–1

Cameo glass scent bottles. Upper left and right, center, and lower left bottles are from a private collection. Photograph: Skylight Studio.

ment. The stopper is sterling silver, hallmarked London, 1887. The bottle is attributed to the firm of Thomas Webb and Sons and is 4½″ (11 cm) high.

The other large cameo bottle at the top right in Fig. 8–1 is round and is a rich, deep red with white interlining to give it opacity. A white top layer was applied to the outside and cut back in a wild rose design. This too is attributed to Webb. The simple silver mounting is marked London, 1887. The height is 4″ (10 cm).

In the bottom row, left to right, is a small bottle with white carved flowers resembling impatiens over translucent red. The silver mounting is dated 1894–95, Birmingham, and is also attributed to Webb. It is 2″ (5 cm) high. The center teardrop-shape is made in a slightly iridescent green glass cased in white and carved in a lily plant motif that winds around to the back. The cap is plain sterling silver and the marks are worn and difficult to read. Possibly English in origin, 1880s, it is 3½″ (9 cm) high.

At the bottom right, maidenhair fern grows all around this fine citrine-colored bottle with a delightful butterfly on the back. The silver gilt cap is engraved with the initials "E.C.K." Inside the cap under the glass sealing disk is impressed the Gorham Silver Company hallmark. It is also marked "sterling."

Fig. 8–2

Swan's head scent bottle by Webb.

58

The bottle was made by Thomas Webb of England; the silver fittings were made in America. This late-nineteenth-century piece is $3\frac{3}{4}''$ (9 cm) high.

Webb also created cameo glass scent bottles in the shapes of fish and bird heads (Fig. 8–2). These are prized because of their originality and rarity. The swan's head in the sketch was made in pale blue shading to a dark brown at the beak. The mountings were plain silver or fine repoussé. The swan head measures $5\frac{3}{4}''$ (14.5 cm) in length.

French Cameo Glass

The French cameo glass on the whole had a more earthy aspect in color and design. Many names stand out in this particular medium—LeGras, DeVez, Mueller Frerés, Richard, and others, but probably the greatest of all was Emile Gallé.

Gallé was a master interpreter of nature. He used earth tone colors and was able to develop a very personal and unique style. Sometimes an ocher color

Fig. 8–3

Gallé atomizer, $7\frac{1}{2}''$ (19 cm) tall. Photograph: Skylight Studio.

would predominate, other times a rich gold, but usually there was a warmth even in his cool colors.

An amazing example of the work of Gallé is seen in an atomizer in amber, golds, and reds (Fig. 8–3). The bottle was blown in a warm pinkish golden color that reminds one of a sunset, and over this is a layer of orange-red. When carved back in leaves and bell-shaped flowers, the effect of the reds upon the golds is breathtaking. In different lighting, the bottle seems to take on a whole new aspect. The cutting is very fine, and in such an allover design there is barely a space left for the signature, "Gallé." The atomizer top is not original to the piece. The bottle was made c. 1910 and is 7½" (19 cm) tall.

Another atomizer, signed "Gallé" (see Fig. C-54) has a more subdued aspect. The floral design is less complicated, but it has an elegant simplicity. Brick red was cased over an opaque pale cream background. It is 7" (17.5 cm) tall, c. 1910, with bulb and tubing replaced.

An atomizer with an unusual pump design, with patent numbers for several countries registered on the inner siphon, is probably French but has no dis-

Fig. 8–4

Cameo glass with pump atomizer, 6½" (14 cm) tall.

tinctive marking. It has a layer of purple glass nicely cut in a leaf and vine motif over an opaque white background (Fig. 8–4). From the first quarter of the twentieth century, it measures 6½″ (14 cm) tall.

Val St. Lambert

The largest maker of glass in Belgium, Val St. Lambert has been in business since 1825 and has been consistently known as a maker of excellent glass for the table and home. Naturally, the company has blown lovely glass for the dressing table. Some of the pieces were clear glass cased in violet-colored glass or cranberry glass and other colors. These were usually acid cut in floral designs and were signed with Val St. Lambert, or V StL, cut into the bases by diamond point. At other times, the company had the logo acid etched on the bottom.

A fine example of Val St. Lambert's cameo work is an unusually tall bottle with an atomizer head that was made about 1915. It is light green with a dark green overlay and cut with an upper and lower border effect; on the body are leaves and nuts. "Val St. Lambert" is cut in a diagonal on the side of the bottle.

Fig. 8–5

Beautiful cameo glass atomizer of rust brown layered over a warm orange color cut in leaves and blossoms. Signed "RR" for Richard of France. From the 1920s, the atomizer is 8″ (20 cm) tall.

9

The Late
Victorian Period

During the Brilliant period of glass cutting (approximately 1885 to 1910), the large, elaborately cut cologne bottles with facet-cut stoppers and sterling silver tops came into vogue. A lady's boudoir would not have been complete without at least one of these beautiful bottles on her dressing table. At times they might be part of a large dresser set consisting of hand mirror, comb, brushes, manicure implements, jars of various types, buttonhooks, and more. However, most cologne and perfume bottles were created and sold separately.

The late Victorians loved fussiness in their decor. Homes were decorated with all types of knickknacks, doilies, ferns, and pictures; if one of anything was good, two or three more were better. When looking at photographs of homes from the late 1800s, it seems that hardly an inch of table or wall went uncluttered.

This same theme brought forth the opulent plush boxes that housed relatively simple perfume bottles. Boxes were made with doors that swung open, tiny drawers that pulled open, and doors that flipped up and back. Most of these boxes had cut glass windows set into them to reveal the bottles within. Perfume bottles also rested in wire stands with pin trays and mirrors, and some even came in pretty velour-covered satchels. (Several late Victorian perfume holders are shown in Figs. C-32 and C-42.)

Cut Glass

This type of bottle is rapidly increasing in cost as the demand for cut glass from the Brilliant period grows. On both sides of the Atlantic Ocean, masterpieces were created. Many were cut in geometric patterns while others featured delicate intaglios of flowers, vines, birds, and butterflies. The stoppers, if of glass, were usually round and faceted, or they echoed the design of the bottle.

The silverwork on these bottles could vary immensely. Deep silver repoussé was employed; jewels, often imitation, were imbedded; and tortoiseshell with silver inlaid in ribbons and flowers (piqué) or colorful enameling was applied over machined silver. Sometimes the silver was left plain to set off the elaborateness of the glass. These bottles usually had small inner stoppers, and they, too, might be facet cut.

The glass could be cased or flashed and, when cut to clear, the results were spectacular. Most often, however, clear glass was used because of cost considerations and popular preference.

Another thing to remember about these bottles is that the glass cutter was working on a miniature scale. Cutting the same patterns on a large carafe or decanter would certainly require skill, but imagine duplicating the same pattern on pieces five to ten times smaller. One can appreciate the expertise required to manufacture these items.

When buying cut glass, collectors are interested in the documentation of origin. This is certainly commendable but not always possible. Very few cut glass pieces were marked with the manufacturer's trademark in acid etching. Most of the pieces carried a paper label. The trademarks are also difficult to see in most cases, and, unless a person has a trained eye and knows exactly what to look for, they can be missed. A few glasshouses produced their own silver and marked their silver and glass pieces only on the metal. The T. G. Hawkes Company of Corning, New York, was particularly careful to mark not only their glassware but also their silver. Sometimes they used the block letters, HAWKES, or the three-lobed sign with two hawks facing each other. The Tuthill Company of Middletown, New York, also marked their glass fairly faithfully. Unger Brothers, Newark, New Jersey, marked their fine silverwork with the conjoined letters, "UB." A number of excellent books are available that supply more information about these and other marks on glass. Many are included in the Bibliography of this book.

Fig. 9—1

Unusual overlay cut glass bottle has an atomizer top. The dark ruby glass overlay was cut through to reveal a champagne-colored glass that, when viewed in another light, appears to change to a yellowish green. This signifies that it was blown from uranium glass. The cutting is very well done and hand polished. Dating c. 1900, it is possibly Bohemian. Height 6" (15 cm).

There were so many outstanding glasshouses in the American Brilliant period of cut glass that to single out any one of them is a difficult task. Libbey, Sinclaire, Pairpoint, Dorflinger, and countless others were all cutting exquisite and innovative pieces. It is important for the collector to remember that, whether a piece is marked or not, the quality of the cutting, the beauty of the design, and the condition of the item are of utmost importance.

American glass from the Brilliant period is particularly sought after in the United States. A heavy lead glass bottle, c. 1900, is cut in the strawberry heart design (Fig. 9–2). The stopper is facet cut. It measures 6″ (15 cm) tall.

Typical of smaller American perfume or scent bottles are four examples in Fig. 9–4. Three were made by the prolific R. Blackinton Company of North Attleboro, Massachusetts. This company turned out what seems to be a large volume of scent bottles in the late 1800s. Blackinton produced expertly cut glass, usually quite ornate, and then topped the bottles with superbly designed and decorated silver mountings marked on the neck with the Blackinton hallmark (an arrow through a conjoined "HB"), the word "sterling," plus a serial number.

At the upper left in the photograph is a bottle that could either stand by itself or be worn on a ring or chatelaine. From the base it tapers toward the neck. Its vertical ribs are cut in tiny notched prisms. It is mounted with silver gilt branches at the neck that are attached to a chain. A large turquoise-colored "jewel" is set into the simple cap.

Fig. 9–2

Brilliant period cut glass cologne, 6″ (15 cm) tall. Courtesy of and photograph by Arleta Rodrigues.

Fig. 9–3

Cut lead glass of the American Brilliant period. Overall cutting depicting the buzz star motif with various other designs. The stopper is facet cut; 4½" (11 cm) tall.

Fig. 9–4

Four American scent bottles, three by Blackinton with silver gilt mountings and "jewels." Smallest bottle has 14-karat-gold mount. Maker is unknown. All from a private collection. Photograph: Skylight Studio.

Next, moving counterclockwise, is a stand-up flask with a bulbous bottom cut in notched prisms and diagonal hobstars. The tall, narrow neck is cut in a lozenge pattern, and the fine silverwork with gold wash is very decorative. Typical of Blackinton work, emerald green glass jewels are inserted between decorative areas with applied silver enhancements. A larger green stone tops the cap.

At the lower right is a conical bottle that was cut in rings, diamonds, sunbursts, and straight planes. On the neck is a ring that enables the wearer to attach a chain to it. The rim of the neck is decorated with minute beading. The cap is dome-shaped and set with five ruby-colored marquise jewels, with a high, round stone at the top of the dome. Jewels are set in fine jewelry mountings, and between the stones are delicate leaves, scrolls, and dots applied to the surface. Traces of gold still remain on the silver. It measures $4\frac{1}{2}''$ (11.5 cm) long.

The smaller scent bottle, at the upper right, is cut in a tiny leaf pattern that runs up the six sides from base to neck. The mounting is very plain, elegant gold, marked 14 karat. It has no trademark but was American made, c. 1900.

The great glasshouses in England—Webb, Stevens and Williams, Richardson, and others—were also manufacturing elegant cut glass that is very popular with collectors in America today. Two fine cologne or scent bottles from England are shown in Fig. 9–5, flanking a smaller American perfume bottle. All are clear lead glass, beautifully cut, and fitted in sterling silver.

On the left is a round bottle with an allover, finely cut framed hobstar pattern. The cap is nicely tooled and bears an 1895 Birmingham mark. On

Fig. 9–5

These cut glass bottles have sterling silver mountings. Left and right: English origin. Center: American-made. All late-nineteenth century. Photograph: Skylight Studio.

the right is another round cologne bottle with alternating panels of crosshatching, daisy cuts, and plain. The silver is worked in a floral pattern. Also marked Birmingham, it is 4″ (10 cm) tall.

In the center is a geometrically cut round bottle with elongated neck and plain silver mounting. It is marked "sterling," with no clue to the manufacturer. What makes this bottle particularly interesting is the cork stopper with a sprinkler head inside the hinged cap. The top can be pulled up and the contents sprinkled out.

Silver Overlay

The appeal of silver overlay (or silver deposit) never seems to wane among collectors. Indeed, it acquires new followers each year. The graceful, undulating curves typical of the taste of the Art Nouveau period were successfully rendered in this particular medium.

After the glassblower blew the bottle, the surface was painted in the desired pattern with a special flux and then electroplated with silver. Pure silver or sterling silver was used. Sometimes the silver was elaborately cut and engraved by hand. This process was developed in the 1880s and was most popular around the turn of the century.

Most bottles with silver overlay were made of clear glass, and, therefore, the rare colored glass perfume and cologne bottles still command the highest prices in the market. See Figs. C-10 and C-71. Silver overlay has continued to be made, but its heyday was the period from 1890 to 1920.

A common shape for silver overlay bottles seems to be a round, squatty type with a flared neck, such as the one pictured in Fig. 9–7. The necks were always coated in silver, which helped protect the glass from chipping. Stoppers were usually smaller versions of the bottle. A silver area was frequently left undecorated to accommodate the addition of initials or engraving of some kind. This bottle is impressed in the silver near the bottom with the mark of the Alvin Silver Company, Newark, New Jersey. Alvin was one of the largest manufacturers of silver overlay items in the field of toiletries. This bottle is 4″ (10 cm) tall, c. 1900.

Another handsome American bottle was made in a square shape, tapering outward toward the base, with corners cut to flat panels and completely coated

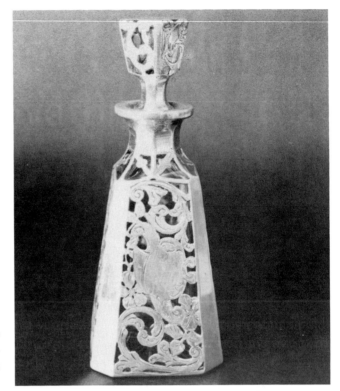

Fig. 9–6

This silver overlay example measures $6\frac{1}{2}''$ (16.5 cm) high. Courtesy of and photograph by Arleta Rodrigues.

Fig. 9–7

Silver overlay bottle is 6″ (15 cm) tall. Photograph: Skylight Studio.

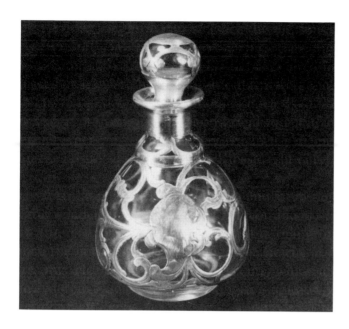

Fig. 9–8

*Fig-shaped silver overlay bottle, 6½"
(16.5 cm) high.* Courtesy of and
photograph by Arleta Rodrigues.

in silver. The floral and scroll design was nicely engraved on all sides (Fig.
9–6). The base was cut in a star and the stopper matches the bottle. Marked
"sterling," it is 6½" (16.5 cm) tall, c. 1900.

The fig shape was another popular shape in bottles. The one shown in
Fig. 9–8 is unmarked, but the stopper and bottle have matching numbers that
prove they were made for each other. It is American-made, 3¾" (9.5 cm) tall.

Sprinkler Top Perfumes

In the unceasing pursuit of inventing ways to apply perfume in a different
manner, the sprinkler top was invented. Tops could screw up or pull up to
allow the perfume to be sprinkled a drop at a time. When the operation was
reversed, the opening was blocked and the perfume sealed.

In Fig. 9–9 are two sprinkler top perfumes of possible German origin, c.
1900. On the left is a violet blue bottle, hand enameled in a white holly
pattern. The sprinkler top is crown shaped. The stopper is gilded, and there
is gold trimming on the bottle. To the right is a deep green, waisted bottle
with gold on the base and shoulder and gold plating on the metalwork. Pink
and white flowers are hand painted over the gold. It measures 3½" (9 cm) high.

Fig. 9–9

These sprinkler-topped perfumes were probably made in Germany, c. 1900.

Rings on Her Fingers

Wearing a scent bottle hanging from a chatelaine was one way to display the scent bottle, but there was another. A woman could also wear one dangling from her finger as she waltzed around the dance floor. If the bottle contained perfume, she could warm it in her hand, bringing out the full fragrance before

Fig. 9–10

A delightful white porcelain bottle is lavishly decorated with leaves, vines, gold netting, and gold frame around the miniature protrait of a lovely young woman who was a favorite model of the Royal Vienna Porcelain Company's artists. Her face was painted on plates, vases, plaques, and here, on this beautiful scent bottle. The painting is signed "Wagner." On the bottom underglaze is the well-known blue beehive mark of Royal Vienna along with letters and number impressed and written. A sprinkler top in the shape of a crown tops it off. Made in Austria, c. 1880, 4½″ (11.5 cm) tall.

she applied it. Of course, if it contained smelling salts, it was handy in case anyone felt faint or swooned.

Materials could vary, but the use would certainly dictate what might be put in it. A very pleasing bottle that was sold as a world's fair souvenir item had two small shells made of mother-of-pearl joined with a strip of brass. A crown-shaped metal cap covered the cork stopper, and a brass chain and ring were suspended from the neckpiece.

Some were solid silver, shaped like a large acorn; some were glass with any amount of gilding and enameling; and some were shaped like hunting horns. Several fine examples of finger ring scent bottles are shown in Figs. C-16 and C-47.

The Glamour of Glitter

The Venetians discovered that adding gold particles to glass batches enhanced the glass with the warm, rich glow of real gold. Naturally, perfume and scent bottles were given this glittering treatment. The Venetian glassmakers also created a pleasing effect by using gold and silver foil combined with small amounts of colored glass. This mixture was pressed into shapes that allowed the gleam of the metal to enrich the glass. They also gathered millefiori canes with tiny portraits in them to create truly exquisite pieces. These are becoming exceedingly hard to find. Another Venetian technique used minute particles of copper in colored glass threads resembling goldstone. These were inlaid while still molten into the equally hot surface of the bottle in floral or other motifs. Examples are shown in Fig. C-72.

In England and America, "spangled glass" and "Vasa Murrhina" became popular in the last quarter of the nineteenth century. Glass pieces were blown then rolled in gold, silver, or mica flakes and finally cased over with clear glass to protect the sparkle. Of course, a glamorous effect such as this had to be employed in scent bottles.

"Mary Gregory" Glass

It is important to know that the numerous items decorated with cute children (and sometimes adults) in various activities—chasing butterflies or birds, picking flowers, and such—all painted in white enamel against colored glass and usually identified as "Mary Gregory" or "Mary Gregory Type," had very little to do with the original Mary Gregory of Sandwich, Massachusetts. Mary Gregory was not known to have painted people. She only worked for the Sandwich Glass Company for about five years and was taught to paint the scenes the other decorators used, which were usually winter scenes of farmyards, plant life, and buildings. She quit working there after receiving an inheritance; unfortunately, she died a few years later.

Possibly because she and her sister were two of the few women ever employed at the Sandwich Glass Company, her name became attached to the enameled pieces produced there (Fig. C-15). In the early twentieth century, when people started collecting Sandwich glass, Mary Gregory was already associated with enameled glass, and when the genuine articles were gone, the antique dealers started selling Bohemian and other European imports with pretty scenes painted on them as "Mary Gregory." Most of the glass decorated in that way is quite inferior to that produced at Sandwich, and the shapes of vases, pitchers, and bottles were not typical of Sandwich. Nevertheless, the legend grew—and the prices along with it.

10

Big and Beautiful

For centuries, Bohemia was an important center for glassmaking. In the nineteenth century, Bohemian glassblowers, cutters, and engravers were setting the standards for the Western world. This tradition of innovation in color and design was carried on into the twentieth century. The pure linear shapes of the early 1800s glass became softer toward the middle of the century.

Coating the clear glass with a thin skin of ruby, cranberry, amber, or cobalt glass is called flashing. The Bohemians used this process widely and engraved through the flashing into the clear glass. Many of the pieces depicted scenes from popular resort areas or deer and castle designs.

The bottles were also layered, and one or two colors might be used. When cut through to clear, the bottle indeed became a work of art. Solid colored glass was also blown into a variety of shapes and could be cut and enameled.

Three fine cologne bottles, shown in Fig. 10–1, illustrate the beauty and fine workmanship of Bohemian glass. On the left is a ruby-flashed, waisted bottle from the mid-1800s. It is decorated with white enamel in a leaf and shell motif, with gold to emphasize the design. The stopper is hand cut and trimmed in matching white and gold.

In the center of the photograph, in striking uranium glass (greenish-yellow), is a graceful cologne bottle fashioned from blown, lead glass. It is cut in scallops around the bottom, with smooth, flat panels that taper toward the flaring neck. The stopper resembles a pointed hat with a scalloped brim. It is hand decorated in ivory enamel and gold roses and scrolls. Probably Bohemian, c. 1835, it is 9″ (23 cm) tall.

Fig. 10–1

Left to right: *Ruby-flashed glass with white enamel and gold. Greenish-yellow uranium glass, blown and cut with white enamel and gold, and three-layered glass, pink over white over clear, blown and cut (could be Sandwich glass). First two examples are probably Bohemian.* Photograph: Skylight Studio.

On the right is an outstanding cologne bottle in pink glass over white over clear. It has an applied ring on the neck and is cut through to give the observer the effect of looking into a room with many wonderful windows. Its origin is probably Bohemia, c. 1840.

Two elegant bottles from France, c. 1900, are large, square, hand blown, and cut (Fig. 10–2). In clear glass, they were engraved with flowers and dec-

Fig. 10–2

Two large French colognes in ormolu stands are from a private collection. Photograph: Skylight Studio.

Fig. 10–3

Two cologne bottles and a covered powder box of apple green opalene glass beautifully enameled in whites, pinks, and greens, and accented with gold. The bottles are about 8″ (20 cm) tall. Probably French.

orated with straight cuts at the bottom. The ball-shaped stoppers are facet cut. The bottles are set into fine gilded mountings with the bases in leaf and crescent ornamentations. Each corner post is in the shape of a torch from which swags laden with flowers are suspended. Impressed "France" in the metal, they measure 8″ (20 cm) tall.

Fig. 10–4

A tall, graceful bottle, deep pink cased over white with matching stopper. Gold has been elaborately used as the only decoration. England, c. 1870, about 7½″ (19 cm).

Another exquisite pair to grace the dressing table is made of tortoiseshell glass (Fig. 10–5). These c. 1900 bottles are most sophisticated, with little adornment because the glass is so richly colored in light and deep amber. The square bottles were blown and shoulders were cut in broad panels. The metal mounts are gilded bronze that encase the base, corners, and shoulder with a suggestion of overlapping ribbons, held by applied diamond-shaped medallions at the corners. The stoppers are cut in flat diamonds and gilded. "France" is impressed into the metal on each base. They measure 6½" (16 cm) tall.

A striking bottle, due to its size and fantastic color, is one that was blown in the wonderful rare color called pigeon blood. This color is seldom seen and is a true glorious red, more toward the orange tint than cranberry or ruby. Since the bottle and atomizer rise to a height of 12" (30 cm), its size alone is arresting. However, the simple flat cuts, which are the only decoration, carry the eye from base to neck. The origin is unknown, c. 1920. This lovely bottle is pictured in Fig. C-66.

Fig. 10–5

These large tortoiseshell glass colognes in bronze stands were made in France. Private collection. Photograph: Skylight Studio.

11

The Innovators

 **Lalique**

Lalique is a magical name in twentieth century glass. The company, founded by René Lalique in Paris, France, in the early 1900s, had become one of the greatest glasshouses in the world by the 1930s.

Using blown-molded and pressed techniques with excellent designs, Lalique was soon producing perfume flacons for Coty, D'Orsay, Roget et Gallet, Rigaud, Vigny, Worth, and others.

Lalique was making not only fine commercial bottles but lovely decorator pieces into which the perfume could be decanted. Matched toilet sets consisting of powder boxes, colognes, perfumes, and trays were also produced by them.

The excellent quality lead glass from Lalique was usually acid-treated to give it a soft, satiny finish, and raised areas were polished to highlight the motifs. This glasshouse used a variety of designs, polishes, and colors in making their highly rated glass, but the lustrous, acid-etched clear glass with the silken surface was and is the most popular. When enhanced with delicate staining to emphasize details, the prices of the beautiful pieces can soar.

Any glass made while René Lalique was alive commands much higher prices than that produced after his death in 1945. Many of his designs continued in production after his death, but the "R" was eliminated from the Lalique mark.

Fig. 11–1

Two R. Lalique bottles made for Corday's "Tzigane" perfume. Both bottles still bear the black stain on the letters. The smaller bottle is 4½" (11 cm) tall; late 1930s.

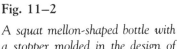

Fig. 11–2

A squat mellon-shaped bottle with a stopper molded in the design of butterflies. This bottle sold without perfume about 1930. On the right is a bottle made for Molinard depicting dancing nudes. This bottle has a pump-spray head. The bottle also was made with a floral stopper. "R. Lalique" is molded into the bottle and acid-etched on base; 5½" (14 cm) high, c. 1930.

For many years, commercial perfumes have been sold in Lalique bottles. Styles range from the early undulating nudes and cleverly sculpted floral themes to today's graceful 'L'Air du Temps for Nina Ricci, easily recognized by the two doves in flight over the swirled bottle.

René Lalique created one of his most dramatic perfume bottles in black glass with straight sides that taper slightly toward the neck. Recessed in each corner is a slender draped female figure. Each figure is in a matte finish, and the flat surfaces are highly polished. The stopper is square, slightly raised in the center, and has a relief design. Pictured in Fig. 11–4, the bottle was made for D'Orsay and marked "Lalique" on the side of the base, c. 1915.

Fig. 11–3

Beautiful frosted bottle molded in the shape of a dahlia, with the center petals stained in black. Original design from R. Lalique, but since this bottle was made after the death of René Lalique, it is merely signed in script "Lalique" and bears a silver and white label on the side. This bottle was sold empty for perfume to be decanted into it. On the right is the 1930s "Imprudence" bottle for Worth. The tiers shimmer with a silvery glow; 3" (7.5 cm) tall.

Fig. 11–4

Black Lalique perfume bottle was made for D'Orsay. Courtesy of Fran Peters.

Fig. 11—5

Lalique also made this perfume tester for D'Orsay. From a private collection.

Lalique made a handsome rectangular tester to contain five different scents by D'Orsay for use in perfume shops (Fig. 11–5). Each well was closed by a flower stopper with a tiny dauber. Incorporated into the design of vines gracing the front is the name D'Orsay, polished to stand out from the background and yet very subtle. The perfume tester is signed "R. Lalique" in block letters on the top. The length is $8\frac{3}{4}''$ (22 cm) long, $2\frac{1}{8}''$ (5.3 cm) wide, by $1\frac{1}{3}''$ (3.3 cm) high. This would date prior to 1945 because of the signature.

Fig. 11—6

Myosotis bottle for the dressing table was made by Lalique in the second quarter of this century.

Fig. C-46

Left to right: *Deep blue glass bottle with white enamel and gold has gilded metal rose shaker stopper; probably German c. 1900. Amethyst glass bottle is adorned with amethyst paste jewels in filigree mountings around base; thistle stopper stretches into a long dauber; Austrian, c. 1925, 7" (17.7cm) tall. Miniature portrait on porcelain, shaker-topped bottle is signed "Wagner"; applied, raised gold motif decorates remaining surface; signed and numbered by Royal Vienna, c. 1875, 5" (12.5cm) tall.*

Fig. C-47

Nineteenth-century scent bottles with finger rings. Left to right: German cranberry glass richly coated with gold and enameled flowers; metalwork is brass; 3½" (8.5cm) high. Mother-of-pearl souvenir bottle with brass mountings. Sterling silver acorn-shaped bottle with screw cap on tiny chain attached to bottle; chain and ring also silver; American. German small green bottle with gold and enameling has gilded brass metalwork. Below: Ruby-cut glass bottle with vinaigrette on wide end; sterling silver and gold plate; English or Bohemian, c. 1860.

Fig. C-48

From the golden era of art glass, three superb examples. Left to right: Round green bottle by Thomas Webb has satin finish, hand-applied gold motif; screw cap is hallmarked "London, 1885"; 3½" (8.5cm) high. Peachblow bottle with floral decoration is also by Webb; silver cap hallmarked "London, 1886"; 4½" (11.3cm) high. Rare creation from Stevens and Williams is in amber swirled glass over mother-of-pearl glass; a greenish iridescence highlights the swirls; c. 1875, 4¼" (10.5cm) high. Private Collection.

Fig. C-49

Fig. C-51

Fig. C-52

Fig. C-50

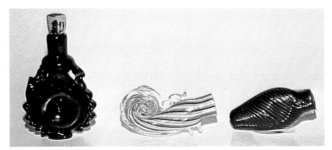

Fig. C-53

Fig. C-54

Fig. C-55

Fig. C-56

Fig. C-49 *Smelling salts in original kid leather purse was a product of Crown Perfumery, London, England, c. 1900.*

Fig. C-50 *Perfumizer by DeVilbiss in pale amber with leaf cut and a long metal stem. Traces of gold remain on metal. About 7" (17.5cm) tall.*

Fig. C-51 *DeVilbiss perfumizers from the Imperial Collection, c. 1925. Left: Outstanding bottle, shading from pink to purple, has applied decoration in old gold color. Right: One of DeVilbiss's greatest creations in an opaque moonlight yellow graduating to blue. Lacy ormolu-type decoration and amethyst "jewels" add further embellishment.*

Fig. C-52 *Cambridge Glass Company made these bottles for DeVilbiss. Left to right: Opaque, opalescent aqua with hand-painted etched basket of flowers. Opaque light blue, acid-etched bottle with motif outlined in black with gold trim. Black amethyst perfumizer with same decoration as center bottle, but trimmed in silver; spray head not original; c. 1925. Courtesy of Jody Speer.*

Fig. C-53 *Early American scent bottles. Left to right: Free-blown deep amber with applied rigaree. Rare seahorse scent with amethyst and white stripes. "Steigel-type" blown scent in cobalt blue, about 3" (7.5cm) long. Courtesy of Fran Peters.*

Fig. C-54 *French cameo glass atomizer with replaced bulb and tubing is signed "Gallé."*

Fig. C-55 *Russian champlèvé scent bottle by Ovchinnikov is from a private collection. Photograph: Skylight Studio.*

Fig. C-56 *These delightful bottles were each cunningly nested in a cagework of gilded brass. One is opaque white glass, and the other is a clear, deep cranberry. Probably French, mid-nineteenth century, $2\frac{1}{4}$" (5.5cm) tall.*

Fig. C-57

Fig. C-59

Fig. C-58

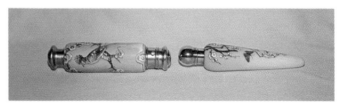

Fig. C-60

Fig. C-61

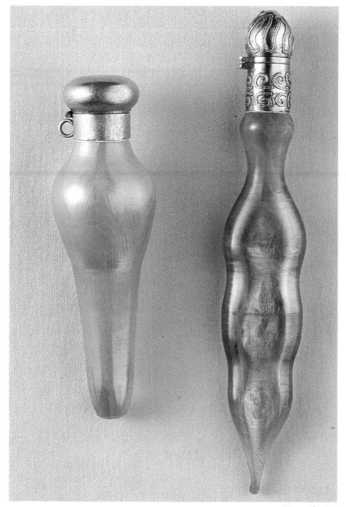

Fig. C-62

Fig. C-63

Fig. C-62 *These two lovely bottles by Louis Comfort Tiffany are part of a private collection.* Photograph: Skylight Studio.

Fig. C-63 *Steuben Glass produced this lovely perfume bottle in a combination of rosaline and alabaster.*

Fig. C-57 *DeVilbiss perfumizer in blue has deer decoration; 6½″ (16.3cm) tall.*

Fig. C-58 *DeVilbiss perfumizer from the mid-1920s is acid-etched, covered with gold, and shows triangles of yellow stained glass edged in black; about 6″ (15cm) tall.*

Fig. C-59 *Steuben made these bottles for DeVilbiss.* Left to right: *Dropper perfume made of gold Aurene glass. Blue Aurene shading to purple at the base. Amber glass with intaglio cut base.* Photograph: Skylight Studio.

Fig. C-60 *Matched pair by DeVilbiss in burnt orange, cased over with clear, satin-finish glass, have Art Deco designs in black; bulb replaced; about 5″ (12.5cm) tall.*

Fig. C-61 Left to right: *Fine double-ended scent bottle has hand enameling, sterling silver mountings; marked "Tiffany & Co.," produced about 1880. Burmese glass bottle by Thomas Webb, hand decorated with "London 1883" hallmark on solid silver cap.* Private collection.

Fig. C-64

Fig. C-65

Fig. C-66

Fig. C-64 *Cameo glass scent bottles. See Chapter 8, "English Cameo Glass," for complete description.* Private collection; photograph: Skylight Studio.

Fig. C-65 Left and Right: *Extremely rare tricolor jasperware scent bottles have sterling silver mountings, "Wedgwood" impressed in bases; c. 1825, 3" (7.5cm) high.* Center: *Earlier circular bottle, Wedgwood blue-and-white; English, c. 1790; 2½" (6.5cm) high.* Photograph: Skylight Studio.

Fig. C-66 *Striking pigeon blood color and 12" (30cm) height make this simply cut atomizer truly arresting; c. 1920, origin unknown.*

Fig. C-67 *Enamel-on-silver scent bottles.* Left: *Mandolin shape has belt hook, gilded silver fittings; marked with "A" and "LP" for Ludwig Pullizer, Vienna, Austria; c. 1880, 2½" (6.5cm) high.* Right: *Pilgrim flask, same markings, silver chain, finger ring; Pullizer was later court jeweler to Shah of Persia.* Private collection. Photograph: Skylight Studio.

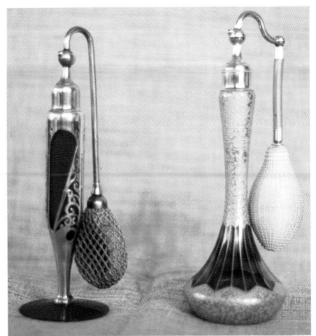

Fig. C-69

Fig. C-67

Fig. C-68

Fig. C-70

Fig. C-68 *Lucretia Vanderbilt perfume was attractively bottled and packaged in this unique silk-lined box.*

Fig. C-69 Left to right: *DeVilbiss opaque red-orange bottle with applied decoration in 24 karat gold is all original. DeVilbiss cranberry glass, acid-etched and decorated in gold; replaced bulb and tubing.*

Fig. C-70 *Two superbly executed, enameled scent bottles were made in France. Left: vermeil mounting. Right: solid gold mounting. Private collection. Photograph: Skylight Studio.*

Fig. C-71

Left: *Deep cobalt blue glass with heavy silver overlay has unusual neck with triple flares; "H.H.F. Birmingham, England, 1910" marked on neck and matching stopper; 6¼" (15.5cm) high. Right: Cranberry colored glass with heavy silver overlay, matching stopper; American, late nineteenth century, marked "Gorham, D 941." Private collection.*

Fig. C-72

Metallic accents supply glamorous glitter. Top row: All Venetian-made, c. 1860. Colored glass globs were joined with foil and pressed into bottles; each about 2½" (6.5cm) high. Bottom row: Three bottles from England. Clear glass, tear-shaped bottle blown with gold and combined with red and blue canes; silver gilt mounting with snap closure is marked "Mordan & Co." Cranberry glass with gold and silver flakes, cased over clear, cut in panels; silver gilt mounting marked "Birmingham, 1885." Cobalt blue glass with blue and pink canes, rolled in silver foil, cased in clear glass; silver cap marked "London, 1897"; 3¼" (8cm) high. Photograph: Skylight Studio.

Fig. C-73

Tiffany & Co. made these flute-cut bottles with long glass daubers; caps are 18 karat gold; c. 1907–1937; 7" (17.5cm) tall.

Fig. 11–7

Commercial bottle by Lalique for D'Orsay has one side with flowers impressed over entire surface, the other side smooth. The center of blossom stopper in block letters reads, "D'Orsay, Le Lys." On the bottom in block letters, "R. Lalique." This bottle is shiny; however, smaller versions are seen with matte areas stained brown or another color and high spots polished. This size was probably used as a display on a counter, c. 1930. It is 7" (17.5 cm) tall.

A bottle made for the dressing table is named Myosotis (Fig. 11–6). Stripes of flowers, accented by colored stain, girdle the sides of the flattened oval bottle, and the stopper is a nude wearing a headdress of flowers and kneeling in a flower bed. It measures 9" (23 cm) high and is part of a four-piece set. Other pieces are a powder box and two smaller bottles with stoppers that portray nudes in various positions. It dates from the second quarter of this century.

Louis Comfort Tiffany

This artist needs no introduction to American collectors or, indeed, to the world. His glass designs were innovative and dynamic. He also designed jewelry, but in glassmaking, his artistry created not only great windows, lamps, vases, and bowls but many small, delicate objects, such as perfume, cologne, and scent bottles.

The silken iridescent glass he named "Favrille" lent itself naturally to ornament fine perfumes. The soft glow of gold so treasured in Favrille glass was made by combining real $20 gold pieces with a combination of hydrochloric and nitric acids and then spraying the solution lightly on the surface of the cooling glass. Gold was also used in the molten batch.

Inspired by the glass and designs of the ancient Middle East, Tiffany reproduced the iridescence that the glass acquired from aging in the elements and even employed the languid shapes of those bottles.

A butterscotch golden scent bottle, which is iridized into hints of pale violet, purple, pink, and blue, was made in the shape of an ancient unguentarium. Feathery lines were formed by quickly drawing a tool through the molten glass. The simple, hand-beaten, golden metal cap has a loop at the back of the collar to enable it to be worn on a chain. The initials "L. C. T." and the number "931" were scratched into the bottom. Made c. 1900, it measures 4″ (10 cm) in length. This exquisite bottle appears in Fig. C-62.

A particularly lovely example of Tiffany's work is a long, flattened scent bottle in bluish tones (Fig. C-62). The bottle undulates to a pointed tip and is capped with an unusual pewterlike metal cap. The neckpiece is longer than the cap and is decorated with scrolled wires soldered to the surface. The cap, which twists and opens back on a hinge, is helmet-shaped with long random loops of the decorative wire. The initials "L. C. T." are scratched into the surface near the top of the bottle along with the number "o8994." The "o" denotes that it was a special presentation piece or gift for a friend or family member. This was made around 1900 and is 5½″ (14 cm) long.

Frederick Carder

Coming from England with a wealth of knowledge about glass from his days at Stevens and Williams, Frederick Carder joined T. J. Hawkes to found the important firm of Steuben Glass Works of Corning, New York. Wonderful colors and shapes were introduced in the early 1900s. Glass, with names such as rosaline, jade, ivorine, celeste blue, and alabaster, was produced in the form of vases, lamps, candlesticks, tableware, and perfume bottles. Steuben's crowning achievement was probably Aurene, to be discussed in the chapter, "DeVilbiss". A Steuben perfume bottle in rosaline and alabaster can be seen in Figs. C-59 and C-63.

Thomas Webb

In England, the firms of Thomas Webb and Sons and Stevens and Williams earned honored places in the annals of glassmaking. Both companies excelled in cameo glass, cut or engraved glass, and art glass.

They produced Burmese glass, which was a glass shading from a pale yellow to a lush pink, by using uranium to make the yellow and adding gold to the heat-sensitive glass to produce the pink color. The glass was often treated with acid to achieve a matte finish. Applied glass ornamentation or enameling was added as further decoration.

Peachblow, a similar creation, was also produced by Webb. Its color is a white or pale gray that gradually moves into a deep pink.

American glass companies, such as Mount Washington and New England Glass Company, were also excelling in the creation of art glass. Competition among the glasshouses of England and America during the last quarter of the nineteenth century was strong, and the world is much richer because of this.

Webb's great contributions are exemplified in the imaginative colors and carving used in their cameo glass. (See Figs. C-34, C-37, C-48, and C-61). This was particularly true after the famous team of George and Thomas Woodall left Stevens and Williams to join the Webb firm. The collector of perfume and scent bottles can find excellent specimens by Webb or Stevens and Williams or the Richardsons and other great innovators, but one must be prepared to pay dearly for these treasures.

Fabergé and Ovchinnikov

The most famous and celebrated Russian enameler was Peter Carl Fabergé. The Fabergé family came to Russia to escape from religious oppression in France. After discovering his knowledge of fine enameling on metals and his ability to execute exquisite designs, the czar issued an imperial warrant appointing Fabergé jeweler to the court. The fabulous works of art produced by the house of Fabergé have since become legendary. Today, Fabergé *objets de vertu* command a "king's ransom" when offered for sale. The enameling on metal created in his studio is perhaps the finest that will ever be seen. No expense was spared when it came to designing gifts for the czar to give to the czarina, his mother, and children or they to each other.

One of the great collections of Fabergé and other Russian enamels is at Hillwood, in Washington, D.C. Hillwood is the former home of Marjorie Merriweather Post, who amassed a great quantity of magnificent pieces while married to Joseph E. Davies, ambassador to Russia in the 1930s. Several fine scent bottles are on display at Hillwood, which is now a museum.

Second to Fabergé in importance was the firm of Ovchinnikov, a goldsmith firm founded in 1853. It specialized in Russian-style pieces and received the Russian imperial warrant in 1872.

A scent bottle created by Ovchinnikov (see Fig. C-55) is unmistakably Russian in origin. The silver bottle is flat and round and decorated in champlevé. To create champlevé, the metalsmith cuts tiny recesses in a design pattern on the surface. Colored enamels are laid into these and then fired and polished to produce a smooth finish. Four different shades of blue were used on this bottle, with white, peach, deep green, and deep red as accents. The round cap unscrews to reveal an inner stopper that pulls out by means of a little loop, which is marked 875 (indicating the grade of silver). The stopper is a cork held between two silver disks. The Russian double eagle mark, symbolizing the imperial warrant, is impressed on the bottom of the bottle with the Ovchinnikov name. It is $2\frac{1}{8}''$ (5.3 cm) high.

Ludwig Moser and Son

As previously mentioned, some of the great glasshouses were in Bohemia. The Moser firm was prominent in the last half of the nineteenth century and is still in business today in what is now Czechoslovakia.

Known for excellent blown glass, beautifully cut and exceptionally enameled, Moser glass in tableware, art glass, and scent bottles is highly prized. A great deal of work is attributed to Moser, especially in enameled scent bottles, but, without a signature or initials, it is difficult to give absolute attribution. However, some unmarked enameled pieces of such perfection have been discovered that left little doubt they were Moser's work.

Pictured in Fig. 11–8 is a fine pair of Moser bottles in amber glass. They are acid-etched about the bases in a vine and leaf design. Above that is etched

Fig. 11–8

Moser created this atomizer and bottle with dropper as a set in amber glass.

the famous Moser Amazon pattern. The vine pattern is repeated on the stopper with its long dropper. Subdued antique gold is applied to the etched portions and in stripes down the sides. These bottles are approximately 6″ (15 cm) tall.

Josiah Wedgwood

In the field of ceramics, hardly any name is more well known than that of Wedgwood. Today, more than two-and-a-half centuries after the birth of Josiah Wedgwood in the Midlands of England, the firm is still producing fine dinnerware and accessory items.

Josiah Wedgwood perfected Queen's ware in 1760, and the pottery has produced it continuously up to the present. Wedgwood also made a dramatic black basalt ware, bone china and many colorfully glazed pieces, but the Wedgwood name is probably most often associated with their familiar jasperware. Jasperware is a fine-grained, unglazed, solid-colored pottery. The applied decoration on jasperware is usually white and features classical motifs and faces and figures from history or mythology. The designs are carefully sculpted and detailed, and, even though in low relief, they give the impression of having great dimension.

When one thinks of jasperware, the soft, medium blue color that has become known as "Wedgwood blue" usually comes to mind. However, Wedgwood also made jasperware in black, yellow, lavender, and green. In Figs. C-44 and C-65, some rarities in these colors are shown that exemplify the great care and artistry Wedgwood put into their production. The soft, silky finish that can be felt on these early Wedgwood pieces may never be achieved again. Scent bottles of late eighteenth and early nineteenth century Wedgwood jasperware are most sought after and very expensive to purchase.

Most, but not all, early Wedgwood jasperware was marked with the distinctive name pressed into the piece. Very excellent jasperware pieces were manufactured by other English companies, such as Adams and Turner, that could be mistaken for the Wedgwood production. Rather poor copies were also produced in Germany during the nineteenth century, but those are easily recognized.

John Turner

John Turner was a contemporary of Josiah Wedgwood who was also manufacturing fine stoneware and jasperware. One of the rare Turner scent bottles from the eighteenth century is shown with two Wedgwood pieces. (See Fig. C-44.)

French Enameled Scents

In the art of enameling, France has certainly produced outstandingly beautiful examples admired by all of the world. This is exemplified in two lovely scent bottles shown in Fig. C-70.

One bottle was made in a flat teardrop shape, with a glass inner bottle coated over and over again in clear amber brown. On each side are graceful dancers, whose diaphanous white garments are sprinkled with gold. Garlands of flowers swirl about them and blossoms crown their heads. The cap, too, is decorated with tiny blooms accented with minute points of gold. The vermeil mounting frames the entire bottle with an astounding amount of cutwork and engraving. The silver is hallmarked with the Paris 1848 mark, but no other attribution can be given.

Enameling and the goldsmith's art are in perfect harmony in a brilliantly conceived bottle made in France in the second half of the nineteenth century. Set against a background of gray clouds and waterfalls are cherubs in various attitudes greeting a pair of lovers. The painting is exquisitely done and framed by a finely wrought rose and yellow gold mounting that encircles the entire bottle, which appears to be solid gold under the enameling. Across the shoulder is a garland of flowers and leaves, so carefully and minutely tooled that they catch the light like jewels. There are scroll appendages at each side to accommodate a chain if desired. A collar with engraving and cutwork extends upward to a rounded neck with stars cut into the gold. The hinged cap (completely lined in gold) displays a dainty setting resembling a crown. Rising from that is the round enameled top with pink roses and a bird in flight at the very top. On the back is an equally lovely painting of a young woman and two cherubs. The gold bears the Paris 1848 guarantee mark. The length is $3\frac{1}{3}''$ (8.33 cm). Made in the second half of the nineteenth century, this beauty is from a private collection.

12

DeVilbiss

"A drop of perfume bursting into myriad atoms of fragrance makes the use of perfume an added delight." This was the poetic description used by the DeVilbiss Company of Toledo, Ohio, to promote the sale of their exquisite perfumizers.

From the early 1900s to the middle of this century, DeVilbiss reigned supreme in the manufacture of perfume atomizers in the United States. The golden years were the 1920s, when they hired the most prestigious glasshouses to supply them with fine bottles to be fitted with their spray mountings or droppers designed by Frederic Vuillemenot.

DeVilbiss purchased glass from Steuben, Durand, Daum, Imperial, and many of the other great glasshouses of the world. The glass was variously acid-etched, cut back in cameo style, jeweled, stenciled, enameled, cut, decorated in 22-karat gold, and mounted with DeVilbiss hardware. They are as beautiful now as they were originally and probably are the most sought after perfume bottles in America today. See Figs. C-11, C-12, C-50, C-51, C-52, C-57, C-58, and C-69 for a number of excellent examples.

The spray bottles currently for sale are made of plastic and are handy for carrying in purse or pocket. They seldom leak, do not break, are not pretty, and one cannot help but lament the passing of the elegant atomizers of the past. The photographs in this chapter show the diversity and grace of the golden age of DeVilbiss. All of the atomizers shown in this book have the original hardware, and many of the perfumizers (as DeVilbiss called their atomizers) still retain their original bulbs and hoses. Some of the rubber, hardened or rotted with age and crumbled away, has been replaced. The bulbs were hand

Fig. 12–1

DeVilbiss perfumizer in orange and clear glass with black and gold trim.

crocheted for DeVilbiss, and most collectors prefer to purchase them intact, if possible. Those who wish to use their atomizers, and many people do, find that the rubber parts can and must be replaced.

A popular DeVilbiss shape had an oval body and narrow stem set on a wide base, such as the beautiful piece shown in Fig. 12–1. The clear, satin-finished glass allows the interior orange color to show through. Bottles were painted on the interior to achieve this soft, glowing effect. Black enamel outlined in gold was selected to decorate the upper part of this bottle, and a gold ring encircles the foot. This bottle has its original black bulb and tube. "DeVilbiss," in gold script, is signed on the bottom. Its height is 7″ (17.5 cm).

DeVilbiss scored again with a delicate pink glass bottle, forever the joyful burden of the golden woman who forms the stem (Fig. 12–2). This is very

Fig. 12–2

DeVilbiss perfumizer in pink glass with gilded caryatid for stem. Courtesy of and photograph by Arleta Rodrigues.

rare, very beautiful, and in excellent condition. The collar decoration is sharp and deep, and the arching metal tube draws the eye down to the beautifully draped figure. Signed "DeVilbiss" in script on the base, it is $7\frac{1}{4}''$ (18.5 cm) tall and was made c. 1928.

An acid-etched body on the atomizer in Fig. 12–3 tapers toward the foot and is coated in gold. Clear yellowish reserves, in teardrop shapes on the sides and encircling the foot, are decorated in shallow cut leaves and flowers. Signed "DeVilbiss" on the base, it is 7" (17.5 cm) tall.

Four DeVilbiss perfume containers typical of the 1925 to 1930 years are pictured in Fig. 12–4. At the far left is a perfume dropper. Its dauber is plated

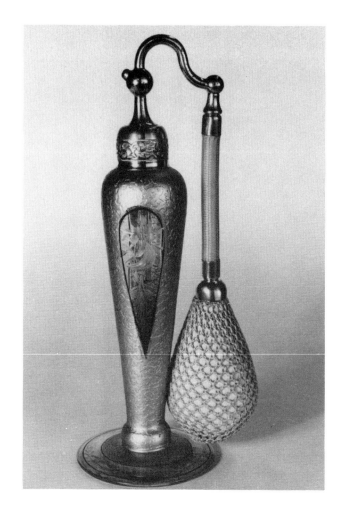

Fig. 12–3

Perfumizer by DeVilbiss in acid-etched glass covered with gold. Clear yellowish teardrop reserves on the sides and a circular ring around the foot are cut in floral motif. It is 7" (17.5 cm) tall, c. 1925. Courtesy of and photograph by Arleta Rodrigues.

Fig. 12–4

Left to right: *Clear glass, blue base with gold leaf design, gold-plated stopper with dropper. Opaque pink with black Art Deco motif. Black perfumizer in Art Deco style, chrome foot, chrome-plated fittings. Opaque blue with gold decoration. All by DeVilbiss. Photograph: Skylight Studio.*

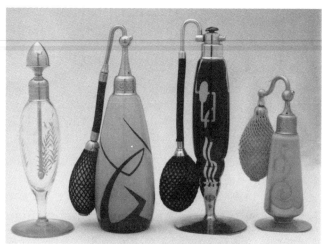

in gold, as is all the metalwork. It extends almost to the bottom of the clear bottle that is decorated in golden fronds. The base is light blue.

Next is an opaque pink bottle with angular black lines that speak clearly of the Art Deco movement. The elongated neck is topped by a spray head and gracefully arching tubing.

A striking Art Deco motif was created in black and chrome by DeVilbiss. Even the spray head has an unusual shape and is capped by a black button making a completely arresting form and design. This may have been marked with a paper label. Its height is $7\frac{1}{2}''$ (16.5 cm).

On the far right in the photograph is a lovely bottle made by DeVilbiss that has charm without the long stem. The glass is opaque powder blue. The only decoration is in gold applied to the foot and base and curving in tendrils up the sides.

DeVilbiss marketed an unusual travel atomizer in c. 1935. The bottle is clear glass with straight polished sides mounted in chrome. The case is black and closes with snaps to form a $2\frac{1}{2}''$ (6 cm) square (Fig. 12–7).

Casting an exciting shadow is another fine Art Deco perfumizer from DeVilbiss. The inverted, teardrop-shaped black bottle swings freely between two winglike supports. The metal is gold-plated. Certainly this is one of the most arresting and original creations produced by the firm (Fig. 12–8).

Fig. 12–5

A gold wreath and stars enhance the porcelain bottle by Lenox for DeVilbiss. The bottle from the early 1930s is moss green and the foot is black.

Fig. 12–6

A DeVilbiss atomizer in disguise. The bottle is a beautiful frosted and polished clear glass, possibly made in France. The tasseled cap lifts off and reveals the atomizer head and bulb. It comes with the original brown leather case that is $5\frac{1}{2}''$ (14 cm); early 1930s.

Fig. 12–7

DeVilbiss perfumizer in fold-up black leatherette case.

DeVilbiss created several dramatic designs in its Imperial Collection. The bottles were ingeniously mounted in ornate metal. Some were jeweled and heavily gilded. They are extremely difficult to find now and are, of course, expensive.

Probably the most popular DeVilbiss perfumizers and dropper types are those made in Steuben Aurene glass, the magnificent, iridescent glass created by Frederick Carder of the Steuben Glass Works of Corning, New York. The glass, usually in golds and blues, was blown into simple shapes and left un-

Fig. 12–8
Perfumizer by DeVilbiss swings between winglike braces. Courtesy of Fran Peters.

decorated because the beautiful glass truly needed no other adornment. Collectors looking for markings will usually find the bases marked with the gold "DeVilbiss" name in script. Sometimes the gold has worn off and no visible mark remains, but, nevertheless, Steuben Aurene and DeVilbiss hardware are easily identified when one becomes familiar with them. The bottles are seldom marked "Steuben," and even rarer are those marked "Carder." However, the shape and the glass itself are just as good as a signature.

DeVilbiss Catalog

DeVilbiss collectors will find the pages that follow particularly fascinating. Reproduced here is a 1924 catalog showing the series of perfumizers, droppers, and perfume lights that DeVilbiss was offering that year.

The catalog itself is elegantly handsome and would have been very expensive to produce, even in 1924. The hardbound cover, in embossed green leatherette, features the DeVilbiss name highlighted in gold. All of the catalog was hand-lettered, and the illustrations are artist renderings, not photographs. Most of the pages in this all-color, hand-bound volume required five different metal printing plates to reproduce the images seen. The DeVilbiss Company spared no expense in creating an impressive showcase for its beautiful products.

Fig. 12-9

Left: White glass, red-orange lined perfume lamp, 7½" (19.5 cm) tall, paper label, by DeVilbiss. Right: Pink and white design on black glass, maker unknown. Both c. 1925.

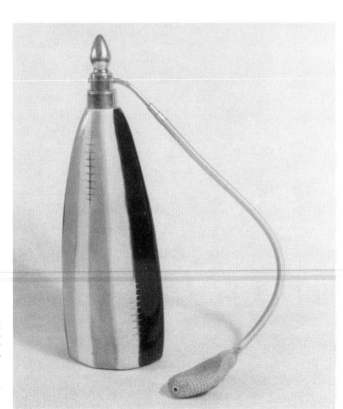

Fig. 12–10

Porcelain atomizer with aqua, gray, white, black, and speckled stripes and hand-applied gold exemplifies some of the changes DeVilbiss incorporated in its last years. Height 10" (25.5 cm), it has gold-plated metal fittings and oval paper sticker on base, "DeVilbiss, S-1790 6, Made in USA." Illustrated in late 1950s catalogs.

Fig. 12–11

Acid-etched, three-piece dresser set by DeVilbiss is coated in gold and hand enameled with pink roses, orange and blue flowers, and green leaves. Tray has $10\frac{1}{2}''$ (26.5 cm) diameter; powder box, $4\frac{1}{2}''$ (11.3 cm) diameter; and perfumizer is 9" (24 cm) tall, c. 1925.

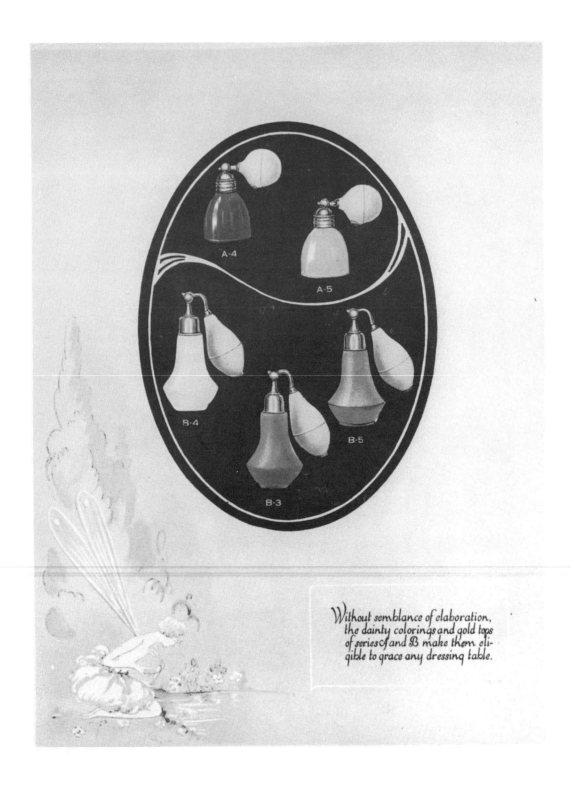

A-4

A-5

B-4

B-3

B-5

Without semblance of elaboration, the dainty colorings and gold tops of series A and B make them eligible to grace any dressing table.

C-8

C-7

C-6

This series achieves distinction —
through the unusual effect of the
pebbled crystal, which scintillates
with glowing color.

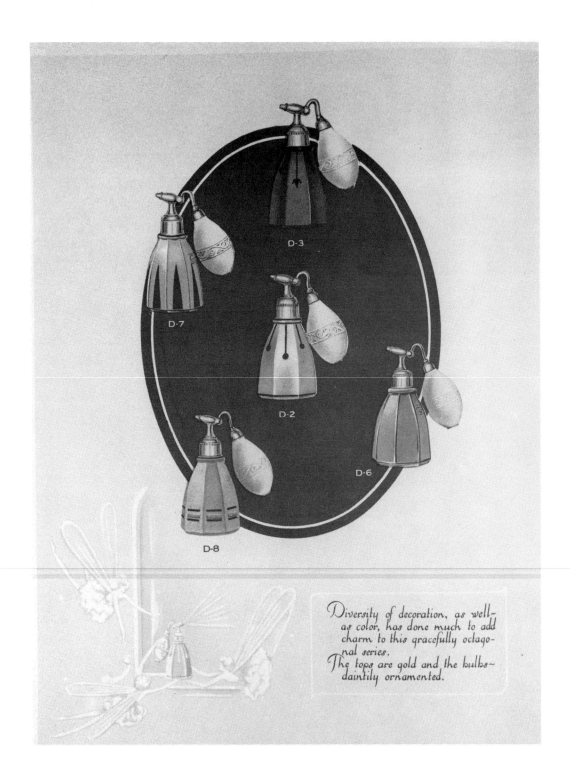

D-3

D-7

D-2

D-6

D-8

Diversity of decoration, as well as color, has done much to add charm to this gracefully octagonal series.
The tops are gold and the bulbs daintily ornamented.

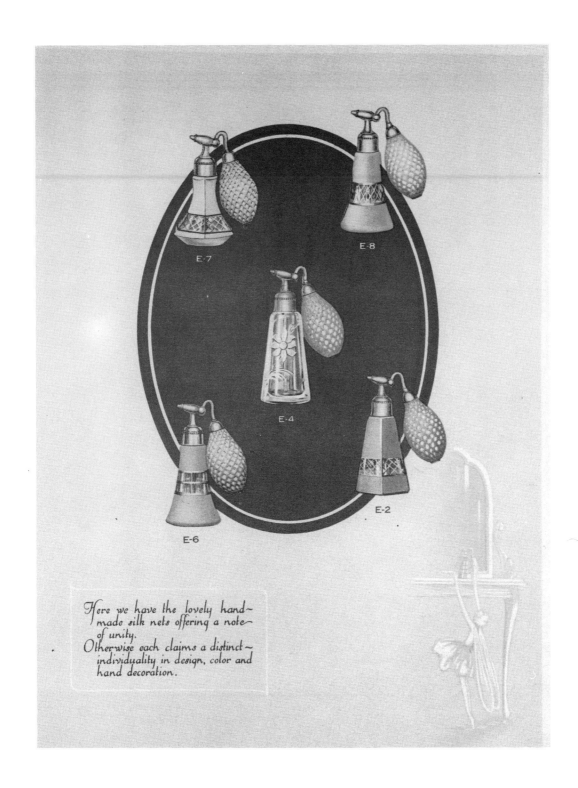

E-7

E-8

E-4

E-6

E-2

Here we have the lovely handmade silk nets offering a note
of unity.
Otherwise each claims a distinct
individuality in design, color and
hand decoration.

F-11

F-5

F-10

F-6

F-1

There is satisfying variety in this series, ranging from a slender, exquisitely etched bottle to a — rather capacious beauty of opaque and clear crystal with gold decorations.

F-8

F-3

F-12

F-9

F-2

A wealth of rainbow radiance
seems to have descended upon—
this colorful series, developed
in emerald, topaz and burgundy.
All of the tops are embossed gold.

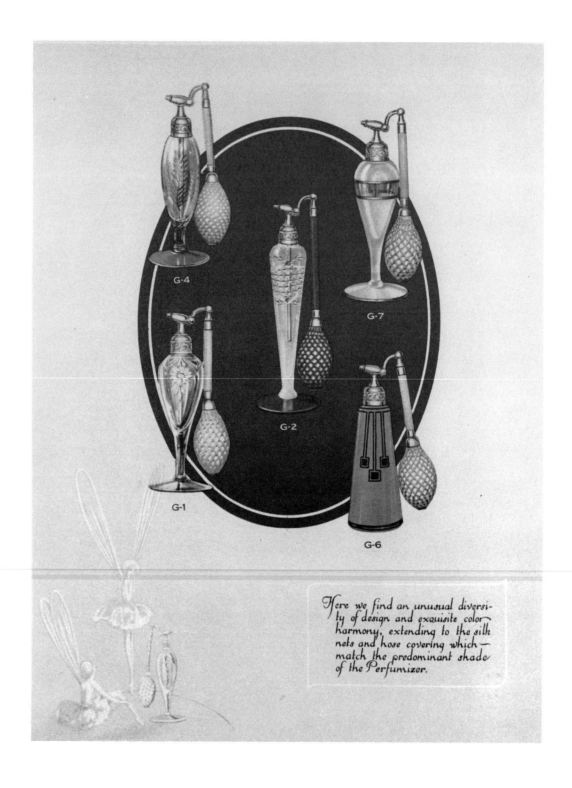

G-4

G-7

G-2

G-1

G-6

Here we find an unusual diversity of design and exquisite color harmony, extending to the silk nets and hose covering which match the predominant shade of the Perfumizer.

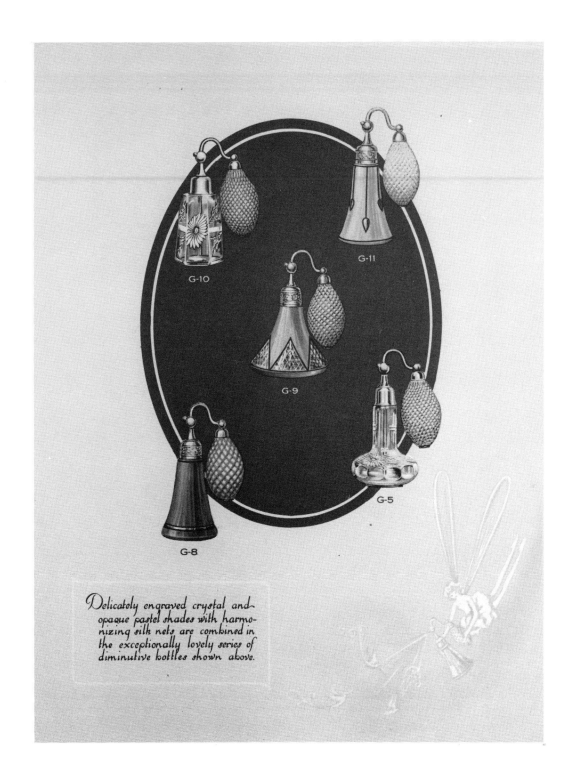

G-10

G-11

G-9

G-5

G-8

Delicately engraved crystal and opaque pastel shades with harmonizing silk nets are combined in the exceptionally lovely series of diminutive bottles shown above.

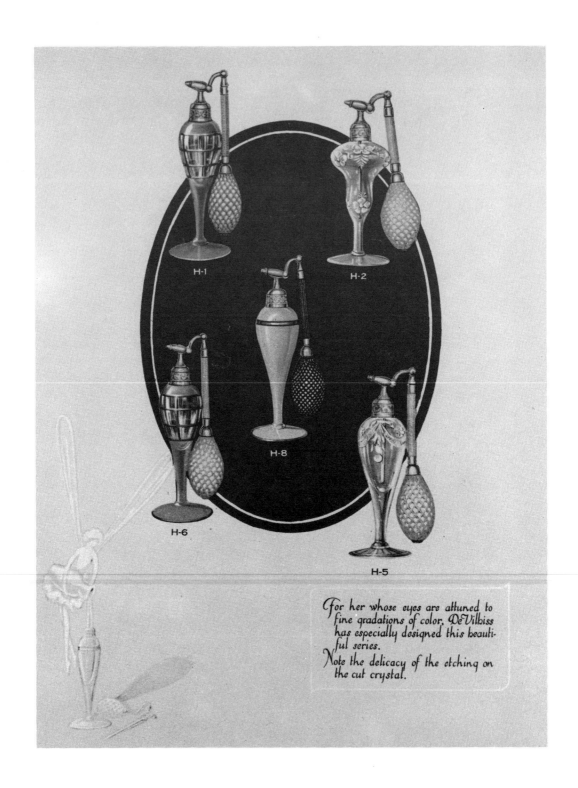

H-1

H-2

H-8

H-6

H-5

For her whose eyes are attuned to fine gradations of color, DeVilbiss has especially designed this beautiful series.
Note the delicacy of the etching on the cut crystal.

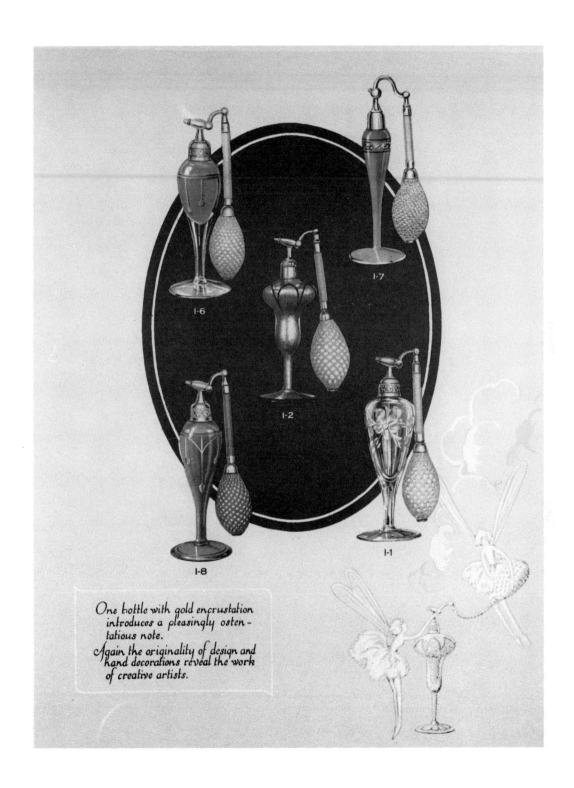

I-6

I-7

I-2

I-8

I-1

One bottle with gold encrustation introduces a pleasingly ostentatious note.
Again the originality of design and hand decorations reveal the work of creative artists.

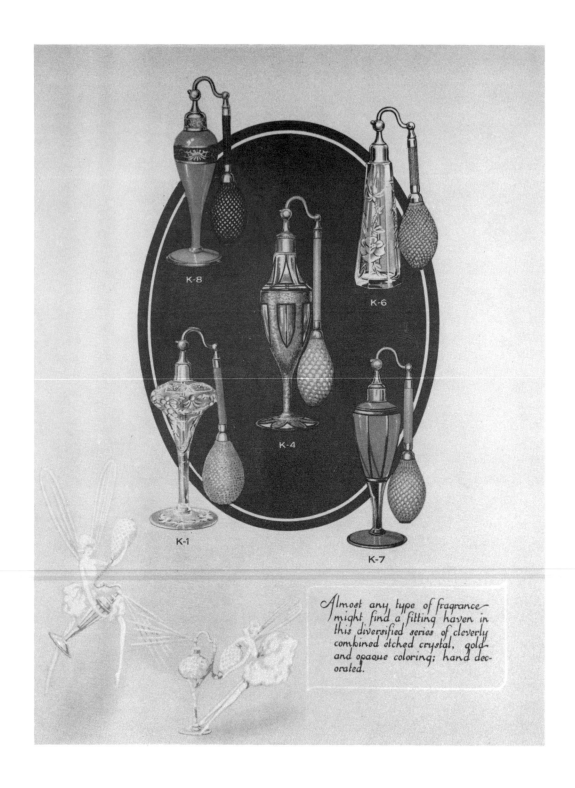

K-8

K-6

K-4

K-1

K-7

Almost any type of fragrance
might find a fitting haven in
this diversified series of cleverly
combined etched crystal, gold
and opaque coloring; hand decorated.

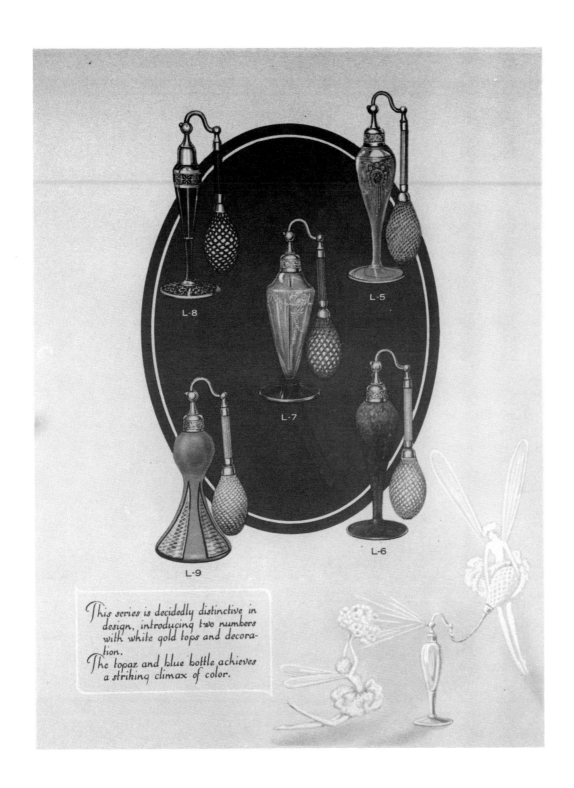

L-8

L-5

L-7

L-9

L-6

This series is decidedly distinctive in
design, introducing two numbers
with white gold tops and decoration.
The topaz and blue bottle achieves
a striking climax of color.

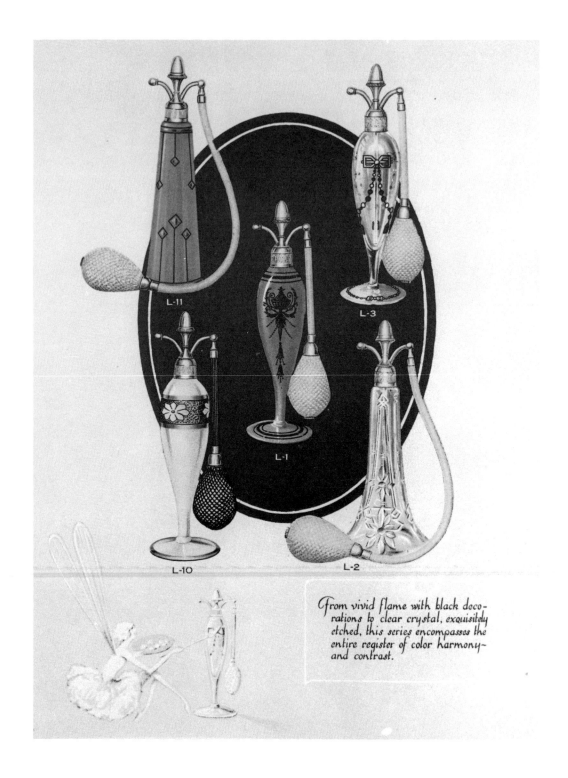

L-11

L-3

L-1

L-10

L-2

From vivid flame with black decorations to clear crystal, exquisitely etched, this series encompasses the entire register of color harmony and contrast.

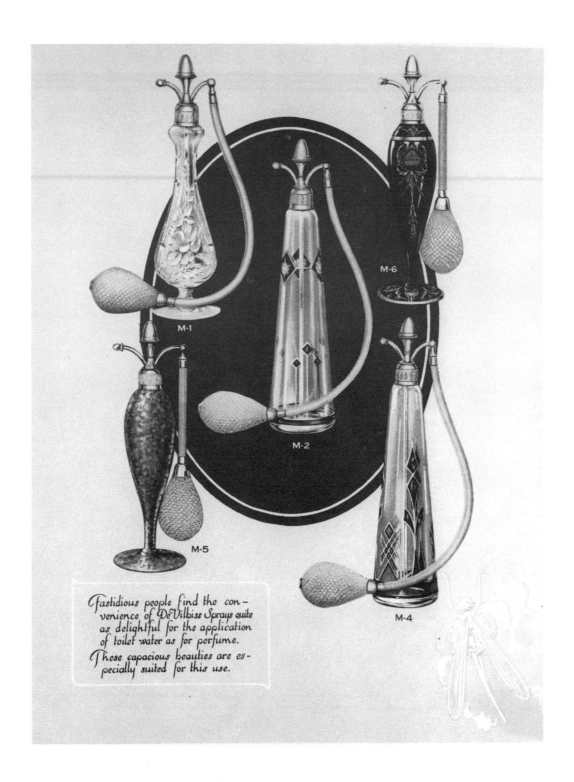

M-1

M-2

M-6

M-5

M-4

Fastidious people find the con-
venience of DeVilbiss Sprays quite
as delightful for the application
of toilet water as for perfume.

These capacious beauties are especially suited for this use.

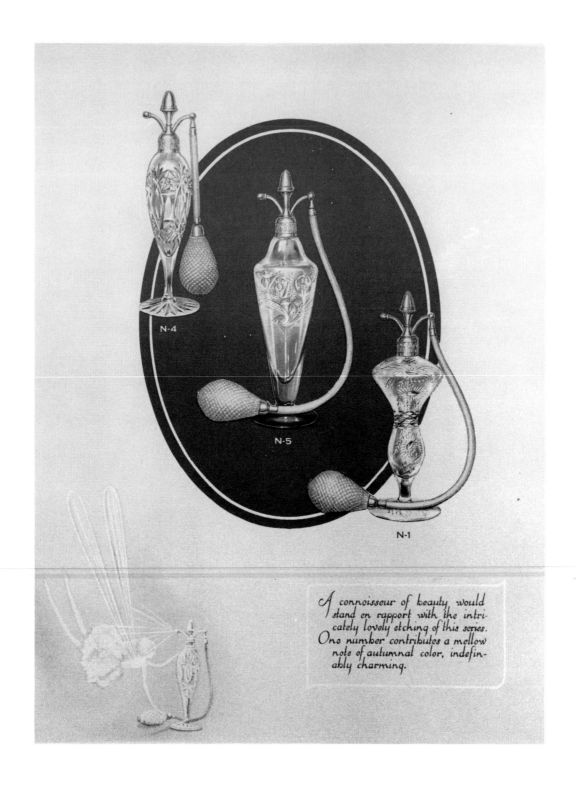

N-4

N-5

N-1

A connoisseur of beauty would stand en rapport with the intricately lovely etching of this series. One number contributes a mellow note of autumnal color, indefinably charming.

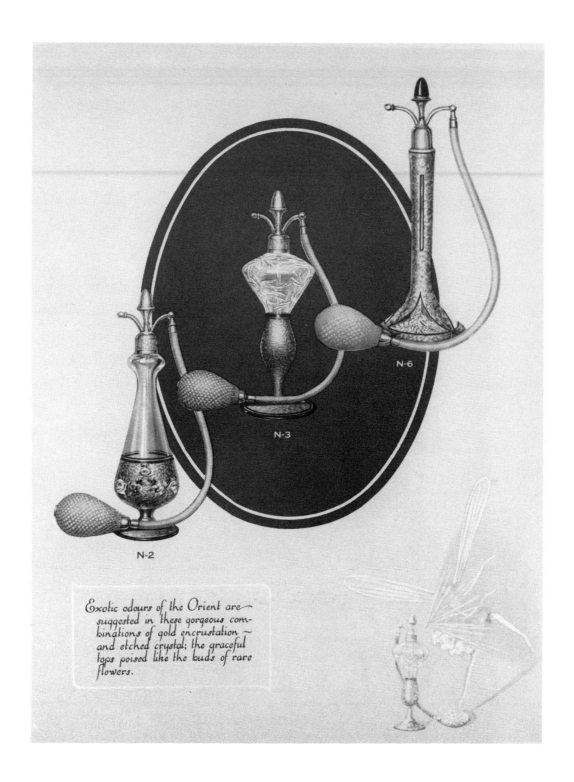

N-6

N-3

N-2

Exotic odours of the Orient are
suggested in these gorgeous combinations of gold encrustation
and etched crystal; the graceful
tops poised like the buds of rare
flowers.

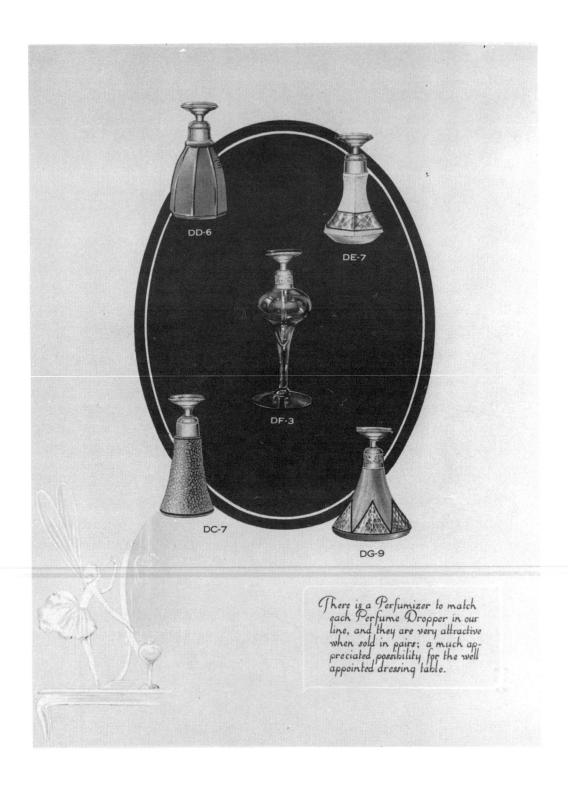

DD-6

DE-7

DF-3

DC-7

DG-9

There is a Perfumizer to match each Perfume Dropper in our line, and they are very attractive when sold in pairs; a much appreciated possibility for the well appointed dressing table.

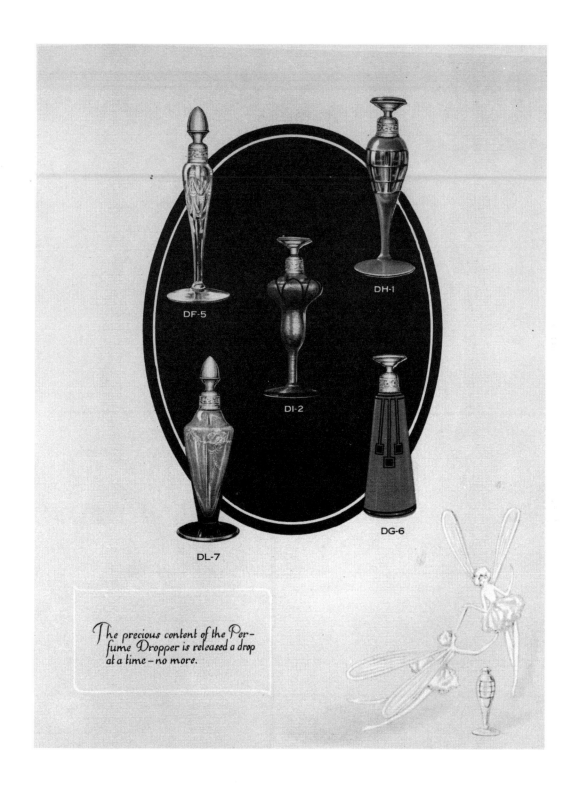

DF-5

DH-1

DI-2

DL-7

DG-6

The precious content of the Perfume Dropper is released a drop at a time – no more.

~ Gentle Light and Sweet Fragrance ~

The gates of one's imagination open softly before
the fragrant, glowing radiance of these exquisitely designed lights.

There are decorations especially appropriate for
boudoir or nursery, and the chalice for a favor-
ed perfume is so placed that the fragrance is
slowly volatilized by the warmth from the ~
electric bulb within.

13

Commercial Perfume Bottles

Commercial perfume bottles, with their limitless variety, are fascinating to collect. The stylish bottles, labels, boxes, and designs all pique collectors' curiosities. Some might be interested in the Art Deco period while others specialize in bottles dating from around 1900. Some may collect bottles and boxes from France, and others might choose only bottles made in America.

Whatever the focus, this is a whole, exciting area for collectors to investigate. The great glasshouses have always been contracted to create dazzling bottles to complement the fragrant contents. Some bottles, such as Chanel No. 5s, were extremely plain, but more often decorator stoppers or figural bottles were the norm.

A favorite among collectors is Caron's Nuit de Noel, with its classic flat black bottle and matching stopper (Fig. 13–1). The label is printed in gold. This particular bottle is $4\frac{1}{2}''$ (11.5 cm) tall, but several sizes were made. The original box is moss green with lighter dot decoration and a glamorous tassel. This was made in France in the 1920s and 1930s.

Three bottles from the first quarter of this century are shown in Fig. 13–2 to illustrate the variety that can be found in commercial bottles. The pressed glass bottle on the left has an elongated neck that accommodates a paper label bearing a carnation plant with two red blossoms and the printed message: "Carnation Toilet Water, Lander, Fifth Avenue, N.Y." The cap is an ocher color made of bakelite. The bottle is $5\frac{1}{4}''$ (13.2 cm) tall. In the center is a white, textured ceramic bottle in a flattened jug shape with handle from the Ricksecker Perfume Company of New York. Pink and blue flowers on a vine circle the lettering on the front, back, and sides. It has a sprinkler top in the

Fig. 13–1

Nuit de Noel by Caron.

Fig. 13–2

Left to right: *Early twentieth century perfumes. Lander's Carnation, cologne by Ricksecker, and Numtax.* Photograph: Skylight Studio.

shape of a rose with a cork sealer. On the collar of the stopper is impressed, "Ricksecker Perfumer, N.Y."

The tiny bottle on the right in the photograph is opaque jade green with a small triangular label in gold and black bearing the name "Numtax." The rest of the label is difficult to read. The glass may have been made in Czechoslovakia.

Roget et Gallet produced a perfume called Violette Merveille at about the turn of the century (Fig. 13–3). The bottle was plain, with the exception of the sides, where each corner was cut to a flat panel and polished. The ball-shaped stopper was facet cut, and the label was embossed with golden garlands framing the ivory-colored center. Rich maroon created the inner frame, and the neck of the bottle was ringed in a decorative paper label. The most out-

Fig. 13–3

Violette Merveille by Roget et Gallet in ornate silk box.

standing feature is its silk-covered box. Gold frames the edges and is embossed into the ivory and maroon silk, setting off the gold garlands and elegantly lettered ivory label. The bottle and box have French stamps applied to them.

Another superb box houses a most exciting bottle (see Fig. C-68). It has a flat, round shape in an almost indescribable color. To call it opaque blue is not enough, but to call it violet is inadequate. It seems to be a combination of the two colors in a marriage that almost makes it glow from within. The stopper resembles a fan, and it ends in a long dauber. Hanging from the neck on a silver chain is the emblem for the perfume that is a silver butterfly with outspread wings in a filigree circle. It has a tassel hanging from it. The bottle was set into a rectangular base covered in silver foil imprinted in blue with the written name of the perfume, "Lucretia Vanderbilt," and the guarantee of authenticity and purity of the product. Equally as fascinating is the wonderful royal blue silk box it came in. It is a real engineering feat. Imitating the case of a nineteenth-century mantel clock, the top is rounded, and the front, resembling a large keyhole, drops open on silken cords to reveal the white silk lining and the striking bottle nestled within. This, too, has a silver base with the signature and guarantee embossed into it. The box will be hard to find, especially in good condition, but the bottle is a little more obtainable, and it is a prize for any collection. The bottle was sold in several sizes, including a small purse size with its own little leather snap case.

Two Hattie Carnegie bottles held Carte Blanch perfume (Fig. 13–4). Stoppers on these bottles are shaped like women's heads with hairdos of tightly sculpted curls. Gilding enhances the name and other raised areas on the larger

Fig. 13—4

Hattie Carnegie bottles. Courtesy of and photograph by Fran Peters.

bottle. The smaller bottle is entirely covered with 22-karat gold. The label on the large bottle reads, "Perfume Carnegie 7 distributed by Hattie Carnegie Inc. NYC Net contents $1\frac{1}{4}$ oz." It is $3\frac{1}{2}''$ (9 cm) tall.

Where else but from France would perfume bottles come that are dressed in their very own designer cloaks? The larger bottle wears an ivory satin cape with gold braid and jeweled trim. A jewel and tiny feather set off the turbaned head made in clear frosted glass. An inner label identifies "Prince Douka," made by Marquay, Paris, France. It is $3\frac{3}{4}''$ (9.5 cm) tall. The smaller bottle wears a green satin cape with less ornate gold braid and a jewel at the neck. Both of these bottles were made in the third quarter of this century.

One of the most popular figural perfume bottles ever made is the dressmaker form bottle made for Elsa Schiaparelli for the fragrance, Shocking Pink. Shock-

Fig. 13—5

Prince Douka perfume bottles. Courtesy of and photograph by Fran Peters.

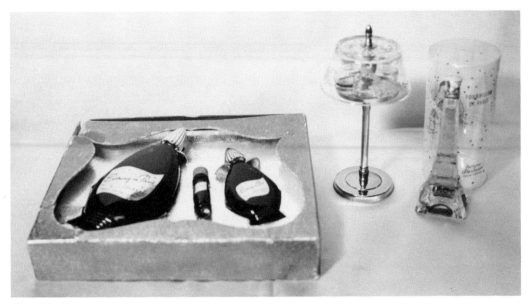

Fig. 13–6

Left to right: *Evening in Paris cologne and purse perfume by Bourjois in original presentation box. Three bottled scents, held by a spring under glass shade of miniature floor lamp, were made in St. Paul; company name obscured. Eiffel Tower bottle from France came in a clear plastic box. All produced second quarter of this century.*

ing Pink just happened to be the color her fashion house was touting at the time. The bottle has a round stopper, and around the neck is a garland of iridescent glass flowers in various colors. A measuring tape with the Schiaparelli name printed on it circles the neck, crosses the bosom, and is held in place by a seal. The bottle, which was produced in various sizes, is protected by a glass dome (Fig. 13–9).

Parfum Orloff was packaged in a glass bottle that was molded in a stylized conception of the Russian imperial double eagle. The clear glass is decorated with a horse and rider shield and marked on the base. It was produced in the second quarter of the twentieth century.

The most frequently purchased perfume in the United States in the 1930s was probably Evening in Paris from the House of Bourjois (Fig. 13–6). It was inexpensive, sold at variety stores, and the little cobalt blue vials could be bought for pennies. It could also be purchased in sets consisting of perfume, cologne, and powder. During the Great Depression, it was one of the few affordable luxuries.

Fig. 13–7

Parfum Orloff. Courtesy of and photograph by Fran Peters.

Fig. 13–8

Each of the delicate blown bottles in this bunch of grapes bears a tiny round label (Violette, Cyclamen, Jasmin, etc.). The original box is decorated in paper of green, gold, black, and white with orange question marks and repeating the name "Rochambeau." Black-and-gold label attached to the stem reads: "Rochambeau Import & Export Co. Contents guaranteed French Perfume." Made c. 1920, the box is 5¼" (13.5 cm) long.

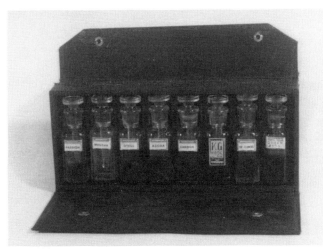

Fig. 13–9

Dressmaker bottle by Schiaparelli.

Fig. 13–10

Perfume stores and drugstores often made their own scents or special concoctions for customers using kits like this one. Assorted scents pictured were labeled Passion, White Lace, Azora, K. G. No. 25, and Queen Bess by Andre Sheron, Paris, France. The pressed glass bottles have stoppers with long daubers that enabled the handler to control the drops needed to create a blended scent. Each bottle is 3″ (7.5 cm) tall. The black imitation leather case, c. 1925, folds and snaps shut.

Fig. 13–11

On the left is Christian Dior's "Diorissimo" in an elegantly simple bottle from the late 1950s. In the center is a frosted bottle with a cutout paper label "Meerts"; with the legend "Flower Dew" on the neck, it appears to be from the 1920s. On the right is LeGalion's bottle for Sortilege in the 1950s; 2½″ (9 cm) high.

Fig. 13–12

A perfume tester for Myrurgia. Six different scents in clear pressed bottles along with stoppers with long daubers are locked onto the gilded plaster base by means of a chrome metal collar. From the first quarter of the twentieth century, the base is 11″ (28 cm) long.

Fig. 13–13

An extremely large man's cologne bottle. Porcelain sea captain in a navy blue coat, white trousers, and red scarf stands on a gray base. The head lifts off at the shoulders. The 12½″ (31 cm) bottle is incised on the bottom with "Dana Perfumes." Third quarter of the twentieth century.

14

Czechoslovakian Perfume Bottles

The Czechoslovakian glass tradition is recognized all over the world for its excellence. Some of the most popular perfume bottles sought by collectors are Czechoslovakian, with their characteristically large, ornate stoppers and fine cut bottles. Most were made in clear lead glass, but some were produced in color, usually pastel, or in a combination of clear and colored glass, as illustrated here.

The bottle in Fig. 14–1 was molded in black opaque glass and given an acid bath to give it a satin finish. The clear flat stopper has an allover foliate intaglio design, emphasized by an amber stain. It was made in the 1920s and

Fig. 14–1

Czechoslovakian bottle in black-molded glass with intricate intaglio-cut stopper decorated with amber staining. Courtesy of Fran Peters.

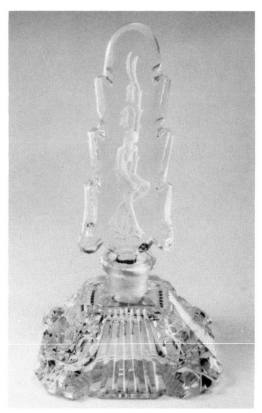

Fig. 14–2

Czechoslovakian bottle in cut glass with intaglio stopper. Courtesy of and photograph by Arleta Rodrigues.

signed in acid on the base, "Made in Czechoslovakia." The height is $5\frac{1}{2}''$ (14 cm).

Another bottle, signed "Made in Czechoslovakia" on the base, tapers in toward the shoulder, is cut on the corners in the "Harvard" pattern, and is prism-cut on the center panels (Fig. 14–2). The tall stopper is flat with bevel cuts on the edges, notched at intervals as it rises to a rounded top. In the center in intaglio is a seated woman beneath bellflowers. Made in the second quarter of this century, it measures $6\frac{1}{2}''$ (16.5 cm) tall.

A bottle in sapphire blue is step-cut from a wide base tapering to the neck and has triangular insets on all sides (Fig. 14–6). A dramatic stopper soars to a peak resembling a skyscraper. Signed on the base, it is from the second quarter of the twentieth century. The height is $6\frac{3}{4}''$ (17 cm).

An intaglio rose with a long stem enhances the flat oval stopper in clear glass, and the shape is repeated in the bottle that is facet and diamond cut on the sides and notched. It is $3''$ (7.5 cm) tall. The acid mark on the base reads, "Made in Czechoslovakia" in an oval.

Fig. 14–3

Jade green elephant bottle. Courtesy of and photograph by Fran Peters.

A green jadelike elephant is an interesting bottle. The Czechs used an opaque glass to make many bottles in innumerable relief forms. Subjects included nudes, abstracts, florals, and animals. The colors were a variety of greens, reds, blues, blacks, and marbleized combinations. The bottles are usually well designed. The jeweled cap on the elephant bottle is not original but appears to be correct. Its height is $2\frac{1}{4}''$ (5.5 cm).

A black bottle molded in a leaf and berry design is decorated on the front with a molded panel of jade green flowers framed in an enameled and gilded

Fig. 14–4

A beautiful bottle resembling lapis lazuli. The opaque blue glass was molded into a scene of a bow hunter and birds. A striking Art Deco period piece. Unsigned but attributed to Czechoslovakia; $5\frac{1}{2}''$ (14 cm) tall.

Fig. 14–5

Czechoslovakian cut glass bottle in oval shape. Courtesy of and photograph by Fran Peters.

Fig. 14–6

Czechoslovakian bottle in sapphire blue cut glass. Courtesy of and photograph by Arleta Rodrigues.

filigree that also encircles the neck. The stopper is a clear molded leaf. It is signed "Czechoslovakia" on the base.

Another small bottle that is probably Czechoslovakian is covered in an allover design of metal leaves and imitation jewels. The leaves are enameled and gilded. This bottle was made in the 1920s and measures about 2″ (5 cm) high (Fig. 14–8; also see Fig. C-20).

Fig. 14–7

Czechoslovakian black molded bottle with clear leaf stopper. Courtesy of and photograph by Fran Peters.

Fig. 14–8

"Jewel" and metal decorated per-fume bottle is probably Czechoslovakian in origin. Courtesy of and photograph by Fran Peters.

Fig. 14–9

Two Czechoslovakian bottles. On the left, the clear bottle is cut to resemble a wide ruffled skirt. The molded stopper in the form of a lady in a long skirt holding a broad-brimmed hat is cut and polished on the edges. On the right, a pink ge-ometrically cut stopper tops a clear cut bottle that spreads out in two lobes. Both are marked with the acid-etched Czechoslovakian mark, c. 1930.

Fig. 14—10

Geometric cut bottle and stopper. Typical Czechoslovakian style of the 1920s and 1930s. Acid-etched on base; 4¼" (11 cm) tall.

Fig. 14—11

Czechoslovakian bottle of pale pink in lobed shape with step cutting and a fancy filigree collar around the neck. The stopper (which may not be original) is molded and polished and depicts a couple from the late 1800s as he is about to kiss her hand; 7¼" (11.5 cm).

15

An Assortment from the Twentieth Century

There are many collectors of pressed glass bottles made during the third quarter of the twentieth century. These bottles are usually sturdily made, and some have tall stoppers resembling the Czechoslovakian bottles. However, these are pressed glass, so they can be purchased at a lower cost than the elaborately hand-cut pieces.

The Imperial Glass Company manufactured many pressed glass perfumes with ornate and large stoppers that are especially popular with collectors today.

Shown in Fig. 15–1 is a container from this period in clear glass with a round, heavy bottle resembling a paperweight. It is stoppered with a stylized bird. The manufacturer is unknown, but it is made in the Imperial style. Its height is $5\frac{3}{4}''$ (14.5 cm).

Another good example of a mid-century perfume bottle has a fancy stopper with an S-shaped plume. On either side of the S are clusters of glass berries. The bottle is decorated with a sunburst in the center and rosette and scroll sides. It is 6″ (15 cm) tall.

Enameling on metal has been a favorite decoration since the French first perfected the technique. In the early part of this century, Americans became extremely fond of enameled dresser items and fashion accessories.

Particularly delightful are the tiny sterling silver perfume bottles with machined designs coated in colorful enamel and often hand painted with garlands of flowers. Sometimes a tiny bird or basket of 24-karat gold would be encased under the enameling. The bottles were usually $1\frac{1}{2}''$ to 2″ (4 to 5 cm) high.

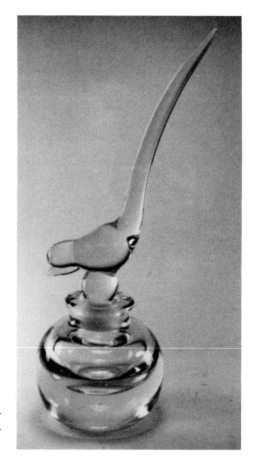

Fig. 15–1

American pressed glass paperweight bottle with bird-shaped stopper. Courtesy of and photograph by Arleta Rodrigues.

Fig. 15–2

Enamel-on-silver scent bottle. Courtesy of and photograph by Fran Peters.

Fig. 15–3

Enamel-on-metal bottle with push-button applicator. Base metal has been plated in silver. Height, 2¼″ (5.5 cm). Courtesy of and photograph by Fran Peters.

Fig. 15–4

American pressed glass with ornate, plumelike stopper is a mid-twentieth century product. Courtesy of and photograph by Fran Peters.

Fig. 15–5

Enameled bottle in flat teardrop shape. Metal bottle is machined with lines radiating from center. Cap is a push applicator that dispenses one drop of perfume at a time. Height, 3″ (7.5 cm). Courtesy of and photograph by Fran Peters.

Fig. 15–6

This wee sterling silver case is the height of elegance. On each side, gray-aqua enamel was applied over machined silver. It has a hinged handle. When the release is pressed, the case snaps open and springing up are tiny tubes, one for lipstick, the other for eyebrow pencil, flanking an equally tiny silver scent bottle. In the other half is a mirror that when lifted reveals a compact. The silver is gold-plated. Hallmarked London, 1924; about 2″ (5 cm) long.

Elegant is the word for the tall perfume atomizer signed in gold on the bottom, "Volupté." This fine specimen is acid etched and coated in gold over a bright orange bottle (Fig. 15–7). The bottle also came in blue and green and probably other colors. It is from the 1920s and is 9″ (23 cm) tall.

Many times perfume bottles came in matched sets consisting of powder boxes and other dresser items. Shown in Fig. 15–8 is a three-piece set in clear glass with black enameling cut through in a very elegant Art Deco design.

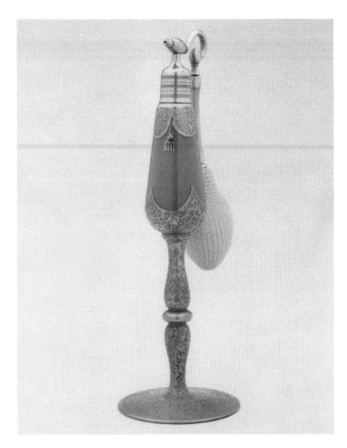

Fig. 15–7

Gold-decorated, acid-etched orange glass atomizer is signed on base in gold, "Volupté." Photograph: Skylight Studio.

Fig. 15–8

Art Deco three-piece set, c. 1930. Courtesy of and photograph by Arleta Rodrigues.

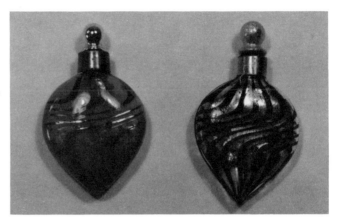

Fig. 15–9

Two bottles blown with stripes of color, with a layer of mercury showing from beneath. Beadlike stoppers have long daubers attached. From Germany, first quarter of this century, 2" (5 cm) high. Courtesy of and photograph by Fran Peters.

Dime Store Novelties

The twentieth century saw the rise of the variety store, also known as the five-and-ten or the dime store. These were stores where, during the Great Depression years of the 1930s, people could buy items from one cent to a dollar; rarely was anything priced more than a dollar. Inexpensive perfumes with titles of flowers, such as apple or orange blossom, were sold in novelty containers that took the form of candles, lamps, animals, and shoes. These could be purchased for about ten to twenty-five cents.

The materials for the holders were made from molded paper, plastic, wood, and metal. Wood containers that held little glass vials inside came in the shapes of bowling pins, dolls, and jugs.

Fig. 15–10

Three wooden perfume containers conceal tiny glass vials. The churn, man, and woman are all about 3" (7.5 cm) tall.

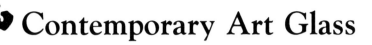

Contemporary Art Glass

Exciting blown glass seemed to disappear during the 1930s and 1940s due to the economic depression and the World War II years. In the 1950s, there came a renewed interest in creativeness with such modern pioneers as Harvey Littleton, Dominik Labino, and Erwin Eisch, who inspired other young people into blowing glass as an art form. It has been thrilling to see this resurgence in glassblowing and the innovative techniques that are being applied to this art medium.

The colors, techniques, and general creativeness of the studio glass movement have brought forth ways to use and perceive glass never before attempted. Some of the greatest glass ever produced is being made today, and who knows what the future may bring? Many contemporary glassblowers are using these techniques in the creation of wonderful perfume bottles. See also Figs. C-1 through C-4.

Fig. 15–11, 15–12, and 15–13

Contemporary perfume bottles showing some of the innovative shapes and techniques incorporated into the late twentieth-century glass movement. All are blown, clear glass with a variety of colored glass used to create exciting accents. At the top, three bottles with interior colors of amber, blue, and amethyst, all acid-etched. Made by Gary Genetti. In the center, four bottles involving a variety of free-form colored glass in red, blue, and amethyst. They are frosted and cut in daring angles. The artist is Joseph Kilvin III. Below, four bottles in a flattened apple shape accented in blues and red. Blown by S.I.N. The bottles are about 3½" (9 cm) tall. Courtesy of D. Erlien Fine Arts, Milwaukee, WI; photographs by Linda Erlien.

Fig. 15–14

Finely engraved sterling silver encases a cobalt blue bottle that can be seen peeking through the latticework. The cap opens to expose the large inner stopper. Made in Birmingham, England, and dated 1912, the bottle is $2\frac{3}{4}''$ (7 cm) tall.

Fig. 15–15

Urn-shaped blown bottle has cut panels tapering up the sides and from the shoulders to the neck. The foot was applied separately and cut with a twenty-four point star. Flat sterling silver stopper by Rogers Brothers has a long dropper. Cap top is decorated with simple stripes and a monogram in the center. American, c. 1920, $5\frac{3}{4}''$ (14.5 cm) tall.

Fig. 15–16

Left: *Cameo-cut bottle in aqua green glass over iridized clear glass. Signed on the base, "Cristallerie de Pantin," with monogram in center, c. 1915, 9" (23 cm) tall. Right: Elaborate bottle in cobalt blue over clear glass, cut in a Maltese cross pattern. Metal fittings are gold-plated. Courtesy of Jody Speer.*

Fig. 15–17

This bottle is beautifully molded to resemble roses, and the stopper is rather abstract. The high spots are polished in the manner of Lalique. Unsigned but most likely Czechoslovakian, second quarter of the twentieth century; about 6" (15 cm) tall.

How to Shop for Perfume and Scent Bottles

Where to buy? Anywhere! Garage and rummage sales are good sources if one has the time. It is occasionally possible to find a bottle or two, particularly commercial bottles, at such sales. Flea markets come in many guises, from junky to sophisticated, and they can be great fun for the collector. One might even find dealers who are knowledgeable about their merchandise. However, be wary about mechandise offered at these types of sales. When "all sales final" is the rule, *caveat emptor* (let the buyer beware).

The condition of the bottle is all-important. The buyer should inspect the item in very bright light because chips, cracks, repairs, and other damage can be disguised by dirt, tape, and stickers in dim lighting.

Auctions are also good sources if you do your homework. Arrive early and preview the material to be sold. Write down the numbers of the items appealing to you and also your price limit. Once the auction begins, it is very easy to get carried away in the spirit of the moment, so resolve to stay within your preset limit. This strategy will preserve your peace of mind and your budget.

Antique shops and antique shows and sales are perhaps the prime source for vintage perfume bottles. The dealers have already been to the markets, auctions, estate sales, and such. The bottles hopefully will have been cleaned and identified before they are offered for sale. Necessary repairs will have been made and noted on the sales tag or brought to the attention of the buyer. Also, people who have collections to sell will often contact an antique dealer to handle them on consignment or buy them for resale. In all cases, the larger inventories of specialty dealers improve the odds of finding delightful additions to a perfume and scent bottle collection.

It is important for the collector to know what belongs together. Sometimes you may see a bottle that originally was cork-stoppered tricked out with a ground glass stopper. Many times the inner stopper for an old scent bottle is missing. This is not a catastrophe. A replacement can be ground by a glass repairer. If the bottle is not actually going to be used as a perfume container, it is not all that necessary. These stoppers are so tiny and delicate, many have been broken or lost. A hundred or more years of age can be expected to take a slight toll.

This is also true of tiny nicks in glass or little dents in silver. If the bottle is rare, beautiful, and one-of-a-kind, it should hardly lessen the value. However, a large chip, crack, or other disfigurement should be taken into consideration when buying. A damaged, rare piece can be a wonderful addition to a collection and often can be purchased at a reduced price. Some items are so unique that, even badly cracked, they still command huge sums. For instance, a rare eighteenth-century Chelsea porcelain scent (the so-called "girl in a swing" type) was displayed by a very reputable dealer with a price tag of several thousand dollars. It had several hairline cracks, but, if perfect, the price would have been much higher.

Another warning regarding repairs: There are skilled people who are able to mend china and other materials with such finesse that it is impossible to detect the repair with the naked eye. Sometimes the work is so delicate that it takes an ultraviolet light to detect it. While skillful repair can save a wonderful item from the discard pile, it poses a problem to buyers. We recommend that you check your sources thoroughly and make sure that all repairs are noted on the sales slip for insurance and investment purposes.

Two problems for the perfume and scent bottle collector are the practice of switching atomizer heads from one make of bottle to another or the utilization of replacement stoppers that are totally wrong and poorly fitting. This is where research becomes important. The collector must understand and learn to recognize the different styles and designs in order to avoid buying these "mistakes." For instance, Czechoslovakian atomizers of the 1920s closely resemble those of DeVilbiss. If the buyer is not aware of the differences, it is easy to be deceived by a married piece. Not all dealers are familiar with the bottles, either. Knowledge protects you from the unwise investment and the uninformed dealer.

A word of caution about purchasing signed pieces: It is extremely important that you know your merchandise; if you are not certain, buy from a trusted dealer. There are unscrupulous people who will take any frosted piece of glass and have it signed "R. Lalique." Not all René Lalique items were signed, especially some made during the Great Depression years of the 1930s. Research the signatures yourself so you can recognize a proper mark. There are people who do nothing but "sign" items with Tiffany, Lalique, Steuben, and anything else requested.

To protect yourself and your investment, buy from a qualified dealer who will stand behind the merchandise and guarantee its authenticity. Study your field of collecting and never be afraid to ask questions. The qualified dealer will be happy to share sources of authenticity with you; he or she knows a satisfied customer will return.

One of the worst examples of this careless marking of items is one this author found in an elegant shop. It was a scent bottle in clear glass with a sulphide of clasped hands inserted into the front. It was perfectly lovely. It had a fine silver mount and was made about 1840. When it was turned over, engraved into the bottom in diamond point was "Steuben." The shop owner was a furniture dealer and had no idea about glass. He thought it was an authentic Steuben and was very distressed to know he had bought a fraudulent piece. Most terrible of all is that this work of art has now been marred forever by someone's duplicity.

Finding information is difficult in this field of study, but perseverance will pay off. Libraries are invaluable sources of information, and the Bibliography at the end of this book should be very helpful. Museums are always interesting, and scent bottles can be found in the most unexpected places. Also listed in the back of this book are a few museums that have collections you might wish to see.

17

How to
Display a Collection

There are many ways to enjoy your collection, depending upon the nature of it. Some are traditional and others are more inventive and ingenious.

The less a piece is handled, the less likely it is to become chipped or broken. Many horror stories are told by collectors who allowed others to dust or wash the precious pieces. Inevitably, something was damaged. You are the ideal person to care for your collection. It is your investment, your pride and joy, and it should be important enough to you to dust or clean it yourself.

A collection displayed on a table or tray requires frequent attention. The alternative is an enclosed space, which can take many forms.

For the small, ornate, lay-down scents, one collector has a lovely Louis XVI vitrine table made of mahogany with decorative ormolu mounts on the corners and feet. The glass top and 3"-deep sides reveal all of the table's interior. The bottles are beautifully displayed on velvet and easily admired without handling.

Another collector has a large, very contemporary, steel cocktail table with a recessed top. The collection can be locked within its airtight compartment, eliminating the need to dust the pieces or polish the metals. It makes a superb conversation piece and creates a sparkling decorator accent in this collector's home.

Another collector uses a partitioned box resembling a typesetter's box with small compartments of various heights and widths that easily accommodate a large number of small bottles. The front is clear glass and the back is opaque glass with backlighting that enables the viewer to enjoy the wonderful colors and shapes.

This same collector has a terrific display area utilizing a wall in her stairwell. Admirers can enjoy the view of her collection in its built-in case while ascending or descending the stairs. The cabinet is 6′ wide, 7′ high, and 5″ deep. Ten

Fig. 17–1

Partitioned box with backlighting to highlight collection. Courtesy of Fran Peters.

Fig. 17–2

Stairwell built-in display area. Courtesy of Fran Peters.

shelves hold an extensive collection of standing perfume and cologne bottles. This cabinet is serviced from the back, which opens into a large clothes closet. The front is entirely glassed in. It takes imagination and know-how to build in such a feature, but these people have plenty of both.

Another display idea is to purchase an antique picture frame and have a 5"-deep box built into the back of the frame. Shelves can be inserted to hold standing bottles, or hooks may be attached for hanging bottles from rings or chains.

These are just a few ideas for displaying your treasures. Actually, the only limitations are space and imagination, so dare to be clever, inventive, and original, but, most of all, enjoy your perfume and scent bottle collection and have fun sharing its stories with your friends.

Glossary

Acid cut back

A process used to decorate glass with acid that eats away or etches parts of the surface not protected by wax or other protective coating.

Art Deco

A period of design dating approximately from 1920 to 1935 that emphasized angular, geometric styles and startling, juxtaposed colors.

Art Nouveau

A late-nineteenth-century and early-twentieth-century decorative style. Typified by undulating, flowing lines, the peacock, and draped clothing.

Aurene glass

Art glass developed by Frederick Carder of Steuben Glass Works in the early 1900s. An iridescent, almost glowing, finish applied to the surface at the furnace by spraying with lead or stannous chloride. Aurene was made in various colors—blue and gold were the most popular.

Aventurine

Glass named after the stone that sparkles with tiny flecks of minerals. Gold, silver, copper, or mica was added to glass in sizes that ranged from minute particles to large flakes. The Venetians pioneered this innovation.

Brilliant period

In American cut glass, the Brilliant period (1880–1910, approximately) is characterized by geometric patterns and deep intaglio cutting on thick lead glass.

Cagework	Decorative, hand-cut, or pressed metal encasing a glass bottle. Not to be confused with silver overlay. Cagework is not applied to the glass, merely over it.
Cameo	The cutting of shell or stone to reveal layers of color in a relief design.
Cameo glass	Two or more layers of glass cut with a wheel or carved by hand to reveal underlayers, as in rock or shell cutting. Acid cut back can also achieve a cameo look.
Canes	Colored glass rods that can be drawn to desired thinness and incorporated into designs, such as millefiori, or twirled and molded to enhance plain glass.
Cased glass	Two or more glass layers of different colors fused together.
Cranberry glass	Deep pink glass made by adding gold and other oxides of metals to the batch.
Enameling	The application of a vitreous compound that is bonded to another surface by firing. Clear or opaque, this form of decoration has been popular since ancient times.
Engraving	Method of decorating glass, stone, or other hard surfaces by means of wheel cutting, diamond point, and stippling.
Etching	Decoration created when hydrofluoric acid applied to glass eats away the unprotected surface.
Favrille glass	An iridescent glass invented by Louis Comfort Tiffany just prior to 1900. Made in a variety of colors, the lustrous effect was achieved by spraying metallic salts onto the surface of the glass while molten at the furnace.
Fire polish	A method of giving glass a smooth, brilliant finish by heating at the furnace.
Flacon	Bottle. French word usually used in connection with perfume and scent bottles.

Intaglio	Method of decorating by cutting deeply into the surface (glass, stone, etc.) of an object at various levels, creating a three-dimensional effect.
Jasperware	Developed by Josiah Wedgwood in the last half of the eighteenth century. A vitrified stoneware mixed with various oxides. Several body colors could be produced. The most famous is the blue with applied white decorations.
Latticino	Thin colored threads of colored glass, spiraled and woven into glass to achieve interesting effects. Originated in Murano, Italy.
Lead glass	A glass developed by George Ravenscroft in England, c. 1675, by the addition of oxide. The result made glass more brilliant, easier to cut, etch, and less brittle.
Mold blown	A process wherein the glass is blown into a mold then reheated and blown to a larger size.
Opaline	Glass that is slightly translucent. Ashes of bones are added to give opacity. Made in all colors.
Ormolu	Brass or bronze, plated in gold, used for applied decoration.
Piqué	A method of decorating tortoiseshell with gold or silver cut into a design that was heated and embedded in the surface.
Ruby glass	Deep red glass made by adding gold and/or other oxides of metals to the batch.
Vermeil	French word for a sterling grade of silver that is coated in gold.

Bibliography

Barlow, Raymond E., and Joan E. Kaiser. *The Sandwich Glass Industry in Sandwich*, Vols. 3 and 4. Barlow-Kaiser Publishing Co., Schiffer Publishing, 1983, 1987.

Bedford, John. *Bristol and Other Colored Glass*. New York: Walker & Co., 1968.

Boggess, Bill, and Louise Boggess. *Identifying American Brilliant Cut Glass*. New York: Crown Publishers, 1984.

Buten, Harry M. *Wedgwood A.B.C. but Not Middle E*. Merion, Pennsylvania: Buten Museum of Wedgwood, 1964.

DeLieb, Eric. *Silver Boxes*. New York: Exeter Books, 1981.

Farrar, Estelle Sinclaire, and Jane Shadell Spillman. *Complete Cut & Engraved Glass of Corning*. New York: Crown Publishers, 1979.

Forsythe, Ruth A. *Made in Czechoslovakia*. Galena, Ohio: Ruth A. Forsythe, publisher, 1982.

Foster, Kate. *Scent Bottles*. London: Connoisseur & Michael Joseph, 1966.

Gaborit, Jean-Yves. *Perfumes, the Essences and Their Bottles*. New York: Rizzoli International Publication, 1985.

Graham, II, John M., and Hensleigh C. Wedgwood. *Wedgwood*. New York: Brooklyn Museum, 1948.

Grover, Ray, and Lee Grover. *Art Glass Nouveau*. Rutland, Vermont: Charles E. Tuttle Co., 1967.

———. *English Cameo Glass*. New York: Crown Publishers, 1980.

Hughes, G. Bernard. *Small Antique Silverware*. New York: Bramhall House, 1957.

Jokelson, Paul. *Sulphides, the Art of Cameo Incrustation*. New York: Galahad Books, 1968.

Jones-North, Jacquelyne Y. *Commercial Perfume Bottles*. West Chester, Pennsylvania: Schiffer Publishing, 1987.

Klamkin, Marian. *The Collector's Book of Boxes*. New York: Dodd, Mead & Co., 1970.

Mankowitz, Wolf. *Wedgwood*. London, New York, Sydney, Toronto: Spring Books, 1953.

Martin, Hazel. *A Collection of Figural Perfume & Scent Bottles*. Vol. 1. Martin: 1982.

Matthews, Leslie G. *The Antiques of Perfume*. London: G. Bell & Sons, 1973.

McClinton, Katharine Morrison. *Lalique for Collectors*. New York: Chas. Scribner's Sons, 1975.

———. *Collecting American 19th Century Silver*. New York: Chas. Scribner's Sons, 1968.

McKearin, George, and Helen McKearin. *200 Years of American Blown Glass*. New York: Crown Publishers, 1949.

———. *American Glass*. New York: Crown Publishers, 1941.

McKearin, Helen, and Kenneth Wilson. *American Bottles & Flasks*. New York: Crown Publishers, 1978.

Newman, Harold. *An Illustrated Dictionary of Glass*. London: Thames & Hudson, 1977.

Phillips, Phoebe. *The Encyclopedia of Glass.* New York: Crown Publishers, 1981.

Random House Collector's Encyclopedia. "Victoriana to Art Deco." New York: Random House, 1974.

Revi, Albert Christian. *American Cut and Engraved Glass.* Nashville, Tennessee: Thomas Nelson, 1974.

_____. *Nineteenth Century Glass, Its Genesis and Development.* Nashville, Tennessee: Gallahad Books by arrangement with Thomas Nelson, 1959, rev. 1967.

Savage, George. *Glass of the World.* New York: Galahad Books, 1973.

Swan, Martha Louise. *American Cut and Engraved Glass of the Brilliant Period.* Lombard, Illinois: Wallace-Homestead Book Co., 1986.

Walker, Alexandra. *Scent Bottles.* Merlins Bridge, Haverfordwest, Dyfed, Great Britain: C. I. Thomas & Sons, 1987.

Wilkinson, R. *The Hallmarks of Antique Glass.* London: R. Madley, 1968.

Other Sources

Go to your reference library and look up articles in periodicals that have been published throughout the years on perfume bottles or perfumery. You can always copy articles to save for your files. Recent magazines to check include:

Antique Bottle Collector, East Greenville, Pennsylvania. Published monthly.

Glass Collector's Digest, Marietta, Ohio. Published quarterly.

Museums

John Nelson Bergstrom Art Center and
Mahler Glass Museum
165 N. Park Ave.
Neenah, WI
Extensive collection of glass paperweights, Bohemian, and art glass.

Birmingham Museum of Art
2000 8th Ave. North
Birmingham, AL

Chrysler Museum of Art
Mowbray Arch and Olney Rd.
Norfolk, VA
Fine collection of early to twentieth-century glass. Ancient to modern artifacts from all over the world.

Corning Museum of Glass
Corning, NY
Outstanding collection of glass with special emphasis on American glass. Large Tiffany display.

Henry Ford Museum and Greenfield Village
Oakwood Blvd.
Dearborn, MI

Harris Museum and Art Gallery
Preston
Lancashire, Great Britain

Hillwood
4155 Linnean Ave., N.W.
Washington, D.C.
Exquisite Fabergé collection and other Russian objets d'art from czarist period. Former home of Marjorie Merriweather Post.

Huntington Galleries
2033 McCoy Rd.
Huntington, WV

Metropolitan Museum of Art
Fifth Ave. at 82nd St.
New York, NY
Porcelain, glass, and paintings.

Milwaukee Public Museum
800 W. Wells St.
Milwaukee, WI
Fine collection of scent bottles.

The Museum of Perfumery
391 Union St.
Aberdeen, Scotland

The Rockwell Museum
Denison Parkway
Corning, NY
Large private collection of glass made by Frederick Carder while he was with Steuben Glass Works.

Sandwich Glass Museum
Sandwich, MA
Extensive collection of local glass with samples from 1825–1907.

Toledo Museum of Art
Monroe St. at Scottwood Ave.
Toledo, Ohio
Wonderful collection of glass from very early, Colonial, and Brilliant periods. Also some rare Lalique pieces.

Wheaton Museum of American Glass
Wheaton Village
Millville, NJ

Index

acid bath, *52*, 127
acid etching, 64, 86, 93
Adams, William, 88
agate, 9, 45
L'Air du Temps (Nina Ricci), 80
alabaster, *1*, 45
Alvin Silver Company (Newark, N.J.), 69
amber flint glass, 38, *39*
amber glass, 86
Amelung, John Friedrich, 35
amethyst glass, 21
ammonia spirits, 55
antique shops, 145
aqua ammonia, 55
aqua glass, *36*
Arden, Elizabeth, *53*
Art Deco, 27, 95, *139*
art glass, contemporary, 141–143
Art Nouveau, 57, 69
Atchison, James, 42
atomizers, 60–61, *87*, 91, *99–118*
  switching head of, 146
"Attar of Rose" bottles, 50
auctions, 145

Baccarat of France, 20, 26
Bakewell Glass Company (Pittsburgh), 36
ballpoint applicator, 48
Battersea (England), 16
Bilston (England), 16
black glass, 26
black jet scent bottle, 43

Blackinton (R.) Company, 66, 67, 68
bloodstone, 9, 45, 46
blown glass, *4*, 6, 141
Bohemia, 21, 24, 75
boot bottles, 51
bosom bottles, 51
Boston and Sandwich Glass Company, 36, 38, *39*
bottles. *See also* specific types of bottles
  shapes of, 6
bracelet, vinaigrette, *11*
brass caps, 21
Brilliant period, 63, 66, *67*
Bristol glass, *14*, 14–16
Bristol Museum & Art Gallery (England), 16
Britain, 24
  chests from, *18*
  vinaigrettes in, 9
bronze wires, 21
Buquoy, Count von, 26
Burmese glass, 85

cairngorm, 12
cameo glass, 6, 57–61
  English, 57–59
  French, 59–61
cameo incrustations, 18
caps, 21
  brass, 21
  sprinkler, 48
Carder, Frederick, 84, 96–97

Carnegie, Hattie, 121–122
Caron's Nuit de Noel, 119, *120*
Carte Blanche, 121–122
champlèvé, 86
Chanel No. 5, 119
chatelaines, 41–44
Chelsea porcelain scent, 48, 146
chests, 16–18
chinoiserie style, 16
Coalport, England, 48
coating, on glass, 75
cobalt blue, 14, *31, 32*
collection display, 149–151
cologne bottles, *126*
   enameled, 77
   French, 76
   mold-blown, *38*
commercial bottles, 83, 119–126
Comyns, W., 42
contemporary art glass, 141–143
copper, enameling on, 16
Corday's "Tzigane" perfume, *80*
"Cristallerie de Pantin", *143*
Crown Perfumery Company, 56
crystallo-ceramie, 18
cut glass, 68
   from Czechoslovakia, *130*
   with uranium, 65
   in Victorian period, 64–69
Czechoslovakia, 120
   atomizers from, 146
   perfume bottles from, 127–133

D.C. Rait & Sons, 24
Dark Ages, glassmaking in, 6
dealers, 146–147
Delft pottery, 27, 30, 31
DeVez, 59
DeVilbiss Company, 91–118
   atomizers from, 146
   catalog of, 97, *98–118*
dime stores, 140
Dior, Christian, "Diorissimo", 125
"Diorissimo" (Christian Dior), 125
display of collection, 149–151
Dorflinger, Christian, 65
D'Orsay, 80, *81, 82,* 83
double-ended scent bottles, 23–25, 48

double unguentarium, *4*
drugstore kits, *125*
Dutch scent bottles, 27–34

Early American glass, 35–40
Egermann, Friedrich, 26
Egypt, 1
Eisch, Erwin, 141
Empire design, *17*
enamel on metal, 85, 135
enamel-on-silver, *136, 137*
enamel scent bottles, 16
enameled cologne bottles, *77*
enameled containers, 9
enameled glass, *33*
enameled scents, French, 88–89
Encyclopedia of Health and Home, 55, 56
English cameo glass, 57–59
English cobalt blue glass, 14
European scent bottles, 13–34
Evening in Paris (House of Bourjois), 123
evening wear chatelaines, 41

F. Hoyt & Co., 48
Faberge, Peter Carl, 85–86
"Favrille", 84
flashing, 75
flask, from Roman Empire, 5
flit gun, 47, *47*
France, 20–22
   cameo glass from, 59–61
   chests from, *18*
   cologne bottles from, 76
   enameled scents from, 88–89

Galle, Emile, 59–60
garage sales, 145
Genetti, Gary, *141*
Germany, 22
"girl in a swing", 48, 146
glass, 13
   Bristol, *14,* 14–16
   coating on, 75
   Early American, 35–40
glass bottles, first, 3
glass stopper, 28
glitter, 73
gold, 27

Gorham Silver Company, 58
granite, 45
Grecian containers, 3
Gregory, Mary, 74
grille, of vinaigrette, 9

hartshorn, spirits of, 55
"Harvard" pattern, 24, 128
Hattie Carnegie Inc., 121–122
Hawkes, T.J., 84
Hillwood (Washington, D.C.), 86
horns, 10, 11
horn-shaped bottles, 52
House of Bourjois, Evening in Paris, 123
Hoyt (F.) & Co., 48
hyalith, 26

Imperial Collection (DeVilbiss), 96
Imperial Glass Company, 135
"Imprudence" bottle (Worth), 81
Industrial Revolution, 2

jade, 9
jasper, 45
Jasperware, 87

Kilvin, Joseph, III, 141

Labino, Dominik, 141
lacrymal vessel, 51
Lalique, Rene, 79–83
    signature by, 146–147
lapel bottles, 51
lead glass, 34, 46, 67, 127
    with uranium, 33
LeGalion, Sortilege, 125
LeGras & Cie., 59
Libbey Glass Company, 65
Limoges, France, 16
lithyalin process, 26
Littleton, Harvey, 141
Longueval, George Franz August, 26
"Lucretia Vanderbilt", 121

malachite, 45
manufacturer's trademark, 64
Marquay (Paris), 122
"Mary Gregory" glass, 73–74
metal, enameling on, 135

metal-mounted scent bottles, 46
mold-blown bottles, 37, 38, 39
Mordan (S.) & Company, 24, 42
Moser (Ludwig) and Son, 86–87
motifs, 7
mourning chatelaines, 43
Mueller Freres, 59
museums, 161–162
My Love perfume, by Elizabeth Arden, 53
myosotis bottle, 82, 83
Myrurgia, tester for, 126

New England Glass Company, 36
Norway, vinaigrette from, 10
Nuit de Noel (Caron), 119, 120
"Numtax", 120

onyx, 1
opal, 45
opaline bottles, 46, 53
opaque glass, 129, 129
opaque white, 15, 15–16
ormolu strips, 21
"Otto of Roses" scent, 51
Ovchinnikov, 86

Pairpoint Manufacturing Company, 65
paperweight bottle, 136
Parfum Orloff, 123, 124
peachblow, 85
Pellatt, Apsley, 19
pendants, vinaigrettes as, 9
perfume application, 48
perfume bottles, shopping for, 145–147
perfume droppers, 94
perfume holders, Victorian, 63
perfumizers, 91
Philadelphia Sesquicentennial, 48
pigeon blood color, 78
pomanders, 6, 6–7
porcelain, 29, 40, 48, 51, 54, 72
    white glass to imitate, 15
Portland vase, 57
Post, Marjorie Merriweather, 86
pouncet, 5, 7
precious stones, 45
pressed-glass bottles, 39, 135
"Prince Douka" (Marquay), 122, 122

quartz, 45

R. Blackinton Company, 66, 67, 68
Rait & Sons (D.C.), 24
Ravenscroft, George, 46
Renaissance, 6–7
repairs, 146
replacement stoppers, 146
repousse, 9, *10*, 11, 24
    in Victorian period, 64
Ricci, Nina, L'Air du Temps, 80
Richard, 59
Richardson, W.H., B & J, 57
Ricksecker Perfume Company (New York),
    119–120
rings
    scent bottles on, 72
    vinaigrettes as, 9
Rochambeau Import & Export Company,
    124
rock crystal, 45, 46
Rogers Brothers, 142
Roget et Gallet, Violette Merveille,
    120–121
Roman civilization, 1, *4*
    scent flask, 5
rosewood, 21
Royal Vienna Porcelain Company, *54*, 72
Royal Worcester factory, 48
ruby glass, 21, 24
rummage sales, 145
Russia, 46

S.I.N., *141*
S. Mordan & Co., 42
St. Amans, Honare and Boudon de, 19
sand core method, 3, 6
Sandwich glass, 74, 76
Sandwich Glass Company (Massachusetts),
    56, 74
Scandinavia, smelling box from, *7*
scent bottles
    definition of, 2
    diversity of, 45–49
    double-ended, 23–25
    history of, 3–7
    materials for, 13
    repairs to, 146
    shopping for, 145–147

scents, history of, 1
Schiaparelli, Elsa, 122–123, *125*
Scotland, 11, *12*
semi-precious stones, 9, 12, 45
sewing chatelaines, 41
shapes, of bottles, 6
Sheron, Andre, *125*
Shocking Pink fragrance, 122–123
"sick glass", 56
signatures, 146–147
silver, 27. *See also* sterling silver
silver overlay, 69–71, *70*
Sinclaire, 65
smelling box, 5, 7
smelling salts, 2, 23, 39, 55–56
Sortilege (LeGalion), 125
sponge box, 7
sprinkler cap, 48
sprinkler top perfumes, 71, 72
sterling silver, 52, *138*, *142*
Steuben Aurene glass, 96–97
Steuben Glass Works (Corning, N.Y.), 84
Stevens and Williams, 57
Stiegel, Henry William, 35
stoppers
    glass, 28
    replacement, 146
sulphides, 18–20
Syrian containers, *3*

T.G. Hawkes Company (Corning, N.Y.),
    64
"tear bottles", 50–51
teardrop shaped bottle, *137*
terra-cotta, 3
testers, 82, *126*
thistle, 12
Thomas Webb and Sons, 57, 58
throwaway scent bottles, 50–51
Tiffany, Louis Comfort, 83–84
topaz, 45
tortoiseshell glass, 78, *78*
trademarks, 64
Tucker Company, 40
Turner, John, 88
Tuthill Company (Middletown, N.Y.), 64
twentieth century, 135–143
"Tzigane" perfume (Corday), 80

Unger Brothers (Newark, N.J.), 64
unguentarium, double, *4*
uranium glass, *33*, 75, 85

Val St. Lambert, 61
variety stores, 140
Venetian bottles, 21
Victoria, Queen of England, 43
Victorian period, 9, 63–74
    cut glass in, 64–69
    glitter use during, 73
    silver overlay during, 69–71
Villemenot, Frederic, 91
vinaigrettes, 9–12, 22

vinegar, healing qualities of, 11
"Volupte", 138, *139*

watch fob scent bottle, *10*
Webb, Thomas, 85
Webb (Thomas) and Sons, 57, 58
Wedgwood, Josiah, 26, 87–88
Wedgwood blue, 87
white glass, to imitate porcelain, 15
William I, king of Netherlands, 20
Wistar, Caspar, 35
Woodall, George, 85
Woodall, Thomas, 85
wooden perfume containers, 140

Price Guide

There is no way to give absolute prices for items as varied as perfume and scent bottles. Retail prices are determined by the weight of multiple factors:

Condition. Is it mint? Slightly marred, scratched, chipped? Is the stopper original?

How Was It Produced? Was it handmade? Pressed? Blown? Mass-produced?

Decoration. Was it hand cut, enameled, stenciled? Also consider difficulty of application. Was metal hand-worked?

Quality of Design. Is it unique, appealing, exciting?

When, Where, and By Whom Was It Made?

Size. Many bottles were manufactured in several sizes. This, too, affects value and, sometimes, rarity.

Supply and Demand. As in all transactions, the most important factor.

This value guide is provided with the reminder that it is merely a *guide*, not cast in stone. Prices vary from one part of the country to another. In a field that is growing in popularity as fast as this one, prices skyrocket in some geographic areas and are difficult to predict.

Color Inserts

C-1, C-2, C-3, C-4 See black and white figures for prices

C-5	Three-piece porcelain set	$750–850
C-6	Porcelain, double-ended	250–300
C-7	Figural porcelain	500–600
C-8	Cut bottle	250–275
C-9	Agate scent/vinaigrette	500–700
C-10	Silver Overlay	285–350
	Cut bottle, silver cap	175–225
C-11	Black suspended bottle	250–325
C-12	Steuben Aurene, tall, extremely rare	1500–2000
C-13	Porcelain, Coalport	600–700
C-14	Amethyst cologne	125–150
	Cologne in brown, amber, extremely rare	400–500
C-15	Enameled, attributed to Mary Gregory	500–600
C-16	Silver filigree, turquoise stones	150–200
	Green opalene	175–220
	Opaque amber, gold, turquoise	500–700
C-17	Sea horse, vari-colored	300–400
C-18	Porcelain flapper set	350–500
C-19	Three-piece Bavarian set	125–175
C-20	Czech Deco bottle	225–275
C-21, C-22	Louis Napoleon scent bottle	Too rare to price
C-23	Two amethyst/clear bottles in stand	900–1200
C-24	Tiffany	400–450
	Others	190–400
C-25	Flashed/clear glass, engraved, cut	275–350
C-26	Bronze goat, aqua bottle	300–400
C-27	Four green bottles	150–275
C-28	*Left*: Cobalt, clear	275–375
	Center: Red, clear, deeply cut	275–375
	Right: Blue/clear	200–250
C-29	Opalene in brass stand	150–225
C-30	Quartz Russian bottle with gold and garnets	Too rare to price

C-31	Triple-layered glass with ivory cap	$550–700
C-32	Victorian plush box	275–375
C-33	Four opalene bottles (see black and white figures for prices)	
C-34	Webb satyr's head in original case	1500–1900
C-35	Porcelain umbrella stand	800–1200
C-36	Jeweled chatelaine	800–1000
C-37	English cameo in case	100–1400
C-38	Miniature perfumes in box	50–60
C-39	Mary Chess set in box	75–150
C-40	Lubin in box	30–35
	Lanvin in box	30–35
C-41	Royal Worcester	150–220
C-42	Victorian brass wire stand, two bottles	175–250
C-43	Russian bottle in original box	35–60
C-44	Two Wedgwood jasperware bottles, each	900–1600
	Turner Jasperware	900–1600
C-45	Agate with filigree top	400–500
	Agate, round shape, gold top	325–425
	Tortoiseshell with stars	400–600
	Mother-of-pearl	225–275
	Viennese dance program	700–900
C-46	Enameled blue with shaker stopper	85–125
	Amethyst jeweled, filigree	275–375
	Royal Vienna with portrait	400–550
C-48	Webb green satin glass, floral decoration	600–900
	Peachblow with floral decoration	650–900
	Stevens & Williams amber/mother-of-pearl	900–1400
C-49	Smelling salts in leather case	60–85
C-50	DeVilbiss in pale amber, metal stem	225–275
C-51	DeVilbiss, pink to purple	275–375
	Gold over pale yellow, jeweled	475–650
C-52	Three DeVilbiss perfumizers by Cambridge, each	200–275
C-53	Amber	250–350
	Seahorse, amethyst and white	250–300
	Cobalt Stiegel type	100–150
C-54	Gallé cameo	900–1100
C-55	Russian champlevé, Ovchinnikov	1000–2000

C-56	Two bottles, one white, one cranberry in cagework; each	$200–300
C-57	DeVilbiss, blue with deer	180–250
C-58	DeVilbiss gold and black	150–200
C-59	DeVilbiss gold Aurene	285–390
	DeVilbiss blue Aurene	425–625
	DeVilbiss Amber glass, intaglio cut base	275–350
C-60	DeVilbiss matched pair in burnt orange	300–375
C-61	Double-ended, "Tiffany & Co."	1200–1500
	Burmese glass, Thomas Webb	700–900
C-62	Butterscoth Favrille	900–1500
	Blue, undulating Favrille	1200–1700
C-63	Steuben Rosalene	300–450
C-64	See black and white figures for prices	
C-65	Wedgwood Jasperware, signed	800–1200
	Round Wedgwood (center)	900–1250
C-66	Pigeon blood atomizer	375–450
C-67	Enamel on silver, mandolin shape	500–700
	Enamel on silver, pilgrim flask shape	450–600
C-68	Lucretia Vanderbilt in case	190–300
C-69	DeVilbiss red-orange with gold decoration	250–375
	DeVilbiss cranberry with gold	175–265
C-70	French enameled bottle, (left)	1000–1500
	French enamel (right)	2000–3000
C-71	Silver overlay over cobalt blue	500–700
	Silver overlay over cranberry	500–700
C-72	Venetian bottles	150–250
	English, colored canes, spangled	250–375
C-73	Tiffany & Co., matched cut glass	750–1000

Black and White Figures

1-1, 1-2, 1-3, 1-4 Historical (prices not applicable)

1-5	Pouncet box	$300–400
1-6	Pomander	Too rare to price
	Pouncet box	300–450
2-1	Norwegian, with chain	350–500
	Cut glass bottles with silver	175–300
	Silver boxes, ornate grilles	250–500
2-2	Vinaigrette, egg-shaped	225–350
	Silver watch fob bottle	375–500
2-3	Bracelet and ring vinaigrettes	2500–3500
2-4	Price not applicable	
2-5	Green agate, horn shape	750–1200
	Animal horn	650–1000
3-1	Price not applicable	
3-2	Early Bristol	400–600
	Blue and white with gold, each	500–700
3-4, 3-5	Chest, French with six bottles	2500–3500
3-6, 3-7	Cobalt in ebony chest	550–700
	Opalene in wooden chest	350–450
	M.O.P., tortoise shell, two bottles	375–600
3-8	Jockey Club set in chest	325–425
3-9	Sulphide portrait bottle	600–900
	Bottle with exterior portrait	350–500
3-10	Red and blue cut to clear (value depends on cutting, rarity, color)	190–300
	Pink over white over clear	300–450
	Striped scents	150–250
	Enameled blue	175–250
	Carnelian, with silver grid	600–800
3-11, 3-12	Prices not applicable	
3-13, 3-14	Plain red with brass caps	125–150
	Plain red with silver caps	140–165
	Fancy cut, silver caps	220–350
	Plain in rare colors	200–300

3-15		Too rare to price
3-16	Lithyalin bottle	$400–600
3-17	Hyalith	600–800
3-18	Dutch, 18th century	175–250
3-19	Dutch, Chinese porcelain, gold cap	450–550
3-20	Mandolin, Dutch, silver	500–700
3-21	Dutch, gold mounts	300–600
	Dutch, Delft pottery	250–375
3-22	French ormolu table with scent bottles	1250–1600
3-23	French, four bottles in stand	1200–1500
3-24	Cobalt bottle	250–375
3-25	Cobalt with clear overlay	250–350
3-26	Cobalt, white, clear	400–600
3-27	Apple green cut bottle	275–375
3-28	Clear, red cut bottle	175–275
3-29	Clear cut bottle	175–275
3-30	Baroque silver bottle	400–600
4-1	Sunburst bottle	125–150
	Cut aqua bottle	150–175
	Aqua, mold blown	75–125
4-2	Clear bottle with rigaree	175–225
	Clear seahorse	135–175
	White striped seahorse	150–250
4-3	Three mold-blown bottles	100–200
4-4	Amethyst, mold blown	175–300
	Aquamarine, mold blown	125–175
	Gothic Arch bottle	90–125
4-5	Pantheon bottle (clear)	135–200
	Sandwich Star & Punty cologne (clear)	200–275
4-6	Seahorse, amethyst, white stripes	225–350
	Lyre bottle	175–250
	"Fountain" bottle	125–175
	Amethyst "salts"	125–200
4-7	Amber cologne	250–375
5-1	Chatelaine, silver	1800–2000

5-2	Chatelaine, jet, carved	$500–700
	Chatelaine, black amethyst glass	300–400
6-1	Bloodstone bottle	500–700
6-2	Figurine with umbrella	225–350
6-3	Flit gun	35–50
6-4	Clown dog	35–60
6-5	Liberty Bell	40–60
6-6	Throwaways, blue and clear	50–75
6-7	Otto of Roses	100–125
6-8	Gourd-shape porcelain	35–65
	Floral top porcelain	50–75
6-9	Engraved bottle	175–225
6-10	Horn shape	150–200
6-11	Silver purse perfumers	60–100
	Glove perfumer	125–150
6-12	Snow man	40–60
	Purse perfumer	25–35
6-13	White opalene	60–100
6-14	Royal Vienna	400–500
	Whippet	500–1000
	Baby in Bunting	500–1000
7-1	Amethyst salts	100–150
8-1	Opaque pink/white	1400–1700
	Red and white (4")	1000–1500
	Red and white (2")	700–900
	Green/white	800–1200
	Citron/white	800–1200
8-2	Price not applicable	
8-3	Gallé atomizer	750–1000
8-4	Cameo, pump	400–500
8-5	Richard cameo	700–900
9-1	Cut overlay atomizer	225–275
9-2	Cut glass	175–250
9-3	Cut glass	175–250
9-4	Blackinton, each	200–300
	Cut with gold mount	350–425
9-5	Large cut bottles	225–350
	Long-neck bottles	175–250

9-6	Silver overlay (large)	$300–450
9-7	Silver overlay (large)	300–450
9-8	Silver ovleray (tall)	375–475
9-9	Sprinkler tops, each	75–125
9-10	Royal Vienna, portrait	400–550
10-1	Bohemian ruby cologne	200–300
	Uranium glass	300–450
	Pink/white/clear cologne	450–600
10-2	French colognes in stand	500–700
10-3	Green opalene set	300–400
10-4	Pink over white	350–450
10-5	Tortoiseshell glass (pair)	500–700
11-1	Lalique, Tzigane (large)	400–600
	Tzigane (small)	300–450
11-2	Lalique, melon shape	600–900
	Lalique, Molinard	700–900
11-3	Dahlia	200–250
	Imprudence	300–400
11-4	D'Orsay "Ambre"	1200–1700
11-5	D'Orsay tester	1400–1800
11-6	Myosotis	1400–1800
11-7	Le Lys	500–800
11-8	Moser set	400–600
12-1	DeVilbiss, orange and black	175–300
12-2	Pink with caryatid	225–300
12-3	Gold with reserves	175–275
12-4	Dropper, blue, clear	125–175
	Pink and black	150–225
	Black and chrome	200–275
	Light blue and gold	110–140
12-5	Lenox/DeVilbiss	80–110
12-6	Frosted in case	225–350
12-7	Clear in case	100–140
12-8	Black, winglike braces	275–400
12-9	Orange DeVilbiss lamp	275–400
	Lamp, flamingoes	240–300
12-10	Porcelain	225–275

12-11	Three-piece set	$400–550
13-1	Nuit de Noel in box ($4\frac{1}{2}''$)	100–125
13-2	Lander's Carnation	20–25
	Ricksecker ceramic	75–100
	Numtax	15–25
13-3	Roget et Gallet in box	125–150
13-4	Hattie Carnegie, large	250–350
	Hattie Carnegie, small, gold	200–300
13-5	Prince Douka, large	125–150
	Prince Douka, small	100–125
13-6	Evening in Paris set	50–80
	Floor lamp	25–40
	Eiffel tower	20–35
13-7	Parfum Orloff	60–80
13-8	Rochambeau in box	100–150
13-9	Schiaparelli dressmaker (large)	150–175
13-10	Case with eight scents	75–125
13-11	Diorissimo	50–75
	Meerts	20–30
	Sortilege	15–18
13-12	Myrurgia tester	250–300
13-13	Dana cologne, large	25–35
14-1	Czech, black, clear stopper	200–300
14-2	Czech, cut glass	175–225
14-3	Elephant jade glass	100–135
14-4	Blue molded	200–300
14-5	Cut oval shape	125–175
14-6	Skyscraper	150–200
14-7	Black with leaf stopper	175–275
14-8	"Jeweled" bottle	125–150
14-9	Cut bottle, lady in stopper	200–275
	Pink, geometric cut	150–250
14-10	Clear geometric cut	150–225
14-11	Cut with pink stopper of man and woman	275–375
15-1	Paperweight bottle, bird	30–65
15-2	Enamel on silver	130–200

15-3	Enamel on metal	$90–125
15-4	Pressed glass, plume stopper	35–50
15-5	Enamel on metal	90–125
15-6	Enamel on silver compact case	500–800
15-7	Orange Volupté	200–275
15-8	Three-piece Deco set	400–600
15-9	Two German mercury perfumes, each	35–50
15-10	Wooden containers, each	25–50
15-11, 15-12, 15-13 Each		250–350
15-14	Silver/cobalt glass	275–350
15-15	Cut bottle, silver top	250–350
15-16	Pantin, aqua green cameo	700–900
	Maltese Cross, blue to clear	450–600
15-17	Molded roses bottle	250–350

DeVilbiss Catalog Pages

100		$25–40
101		35–50
102		35–50
103		50–60
104	F-1, 6, 10, 11	75–125
	F-5	125–165
105		110–135
106	G-1	125–150
	G-2	275–325
	G-4, G-6, G-7	125–165
107		65–125
108	H-1, H-6, H-8	120–150
	H-5, H-2	135–175
109	I-1, I-2,	135–190
	I-6, I-7, I-8	110–150
110	K-1, K-4, K-6	135–200
	K-7, K-8	120–190

111		125–225
112	Tall bottles	250–375
113	Tall bottles	275–400
114	Tall bottles	275–400
115	Tall bottles	275–450
116	DF3	100–125
	All others	35–55
117		135–225